MW01641127

MALANKARA ORTHODOX SYRIAN CHURCH

SHEHIMO
BOOK OF COMMON PRAYER

2016

SHEHIMO
BOOK OF COMMON PRAYER

Published by:

Ministry of Liturgical Resource Development
Diocese of South-West America
<LRD@ds-wa.org>

First Published:

March, 2016
ISBN-10: 0-9972544-0-8
ISBN-13: 978-0-9972544-0-2

With support from:

MGOCSM of Diocese of South-West America
DS-WA MGOCSM <dswamgocsm@gmail.com>

TABLE OF CONTENTS

The Northeast American Diocese
of the Malankara Orthodox Syrian Church
2158 ROUTE 106 • MUTTONTOWN • NEW YORK 11791

By the Grace of God,
Zachariah Mar Nicholovos,
Diocesan Metropolitan

OL No. 22/2015 May 24, 2015

Dearly beloved,

King David, the Psalmist, wrote, "Seven times a day I praise You, because of Your righteous judgments" (Psalm 119:164). According to this ancient model of prayer, the Church has developed a system of canonical offices of prayer to ensure our entire lives are centered on prayer and communion with God. These offices of prayer, otherwise known as the, Shehimo Namaskaram have only been available in Syriac and Malayalam, until now.

We offer our thanksgiving to God, that these canonical prayers are now available in hymn form. The hymnography of these prayers, were developed in line with the tonal system the West Syriac Liturgical Tradition follows. The prayerful and meticulous labors of the younger generation of our clergy in North America have ensured that our rich liturgical tradition is not limited purely to Syriac or Malayalam. Under the mentorship of Rev. Fr. Dr. Baby Varghese, the acclaimed and celebrated scholar of the West Syriac Liturgical Tradition, the prayers and hymns of the Holy Church continue to be translated, and developed.

The work of this team has broken down the linguistic barriers and offered this beautiful treasure of prayers to our English speaking faithful. Through active liturgical translation work like this, the Church has now made Her beautiful worship available to the wonderful people of this land, who are not of Indian descent.

May their work, and continued labors be blessed by the Lord God. May God offer His manifold blessings upon each of them, and their loved ones, for their dedication to Christ and His Church.

As these books are being published by the MGOCSM of the Diocese of South-West America, it is our prayer that the faithful, who are not proficient in Malayalam or Syriac, will use these prayers. May these prayers preserve each of us, as we journey to the Kingdom! May these prayers, bring back our faithful whom we have lost from our Church! May these prayers, deepen our faith in undivided Godhead – the Father, the Son, and the Holy Spirit – One God, forever and ever, Amen!

Yours in our Lord,

Nicholovos

Zachariah Nicholovos, Metropolitan
Feast of Pentecost, 2015

Telephone (718) 470 9844 • Fax (718) 470 9219
www.neamericandiocese.org • NortheastAmericanDiocese@gmail.com

FOREWORD

Shehimo represents one of the spiritual treasures of Syriac Christianity, containing liturgical hymns written since the fourth century AD. Most of the hymns and prayers date back to the first millennium. We have several versions of the Shehimo, of which the version used in Mosul was printed at Mar Julius Press, Pampakuda in the first half of the last century. The Syriac text was translated into Malayalam more than once and the late Mr. C. P.Chandy versified the Malayalam translation, preserving the original Syriac meter. In fact, the credit of versifying most of the liturgical hymns currently used in the Malankara Orthodox Church goes to Mr. C. P. Chandy. He almost always versified these hymns using the same number of syllables as in the original Syriac in order to make the singing of the Malayalam hymns easier and melodious.

Father Bede Griffiths, a former monk of the Kurishumala Ashram (a monastery of the Cistersian Order), Vagamon, Kerala made an excellent English prose translation of the Pampakuda edition of the Shehimo, which was published in the 1960's (Reprint, SEERI, Kottayam, 2006). This is the only known English translation of the Shehimo and is widely known among Syriac scholars all over the world.

Presently, a few dedicated and theologically trained individuals in the United States have taken pains to versify the prayers into English for the use of the members of the Malankara Orthodox Church, whose mother tongue is not Malayalam. This publication is a first attempt at the English versification stemming from these individuals' love for the Syriac liturgy. Experts may have criticisms and suggestions, which are necessary to improve the present work for future editions. I congratulate my young friends and wish them all success for their endeavor.

Fr. Baby Varghese, Kottayam
Feast of Epiphany, 2016

INTRODUCTION

The Shehimo, or the Book of Common Prayer of the Syriac Orthodox Church, contains the daily prayers of the Church. The Syriac Orthodox liturgical tradition observes seven offices of prayer for each of the seven days of the week. According to the Scriptures, the new day begins in the evening and is identified by its number. Thus, the days are recognized as the first day, second day, and so on. This is reflected in Genesis 1:5, **"And there was evening and there was morning, the first day."** The offices of prayer are also referred to as the "Hours". The importance of seven offices is alluded to in Psalm 119:164, **"Seven times a day I praise you for your righteous laws."** The Hours are in the following order:

1. **Ramsho (**Vespers, or Evening), which is observed at 6pm.
2. **Soutoro** (Compline, or Night Protection) at 9pm.
3. **Lilio** (Night Vigil), which is observed ideally in the middle of the night, but often directly preceding the Morning.
4. **Sapro** (Matins, or Morning) at 6am.
5. **3rd Hour** at 9am.
6. **6th Hour** at 12pm.
7. **9th Hour** at 3pm.

Purpose of the Shehimo

1. The primary purpose of the Hours is to praise and glorify God. We were created to worship Him and we will worship Him without ceasing (Revelations 7:15).
2. The seven hours of prayer create a cycle that provides us with a foretaste of the eternal life we will spend in the presence of God worshipping Him.
3. The Hours are a guide for our prayer life. They are instructive and teach us how to pray and what to pray for.
4. The Hours teach us about God and the Scriptures. The Church Fathers taught the Faith and the Scriptures to the common person through liturgical prayers.

5. Each day highlights a specific theme: **1st Day** – Resurrection; **2nd Day** – Repentance; **3rd Day** – Repentance; **4th Day** – Mother of God; **5th Day** – Communion of the Saints; **6th Day** – Cross/Crucifixion; **7th Day** – Faithful Departed;
6. The Hours inspire us to keep our hearts, minds, and thoughts on God. They are a step towards our goal of praying without ceasing (1 Thessalonians 4:17).
7. The Hours fruitfully occupy our time by meditating, reflecting, and developing our relationship with God. If we are praying then we are not sinning. If we spend our time in prayer then we have less time to sin. By keeping our mind on God we are able to fight against sin and separation from God.

How to Use the Shehimo

There has been a notion that the Shehimo is intended only for monastics, but in reality it is intended for all faithful worshippers. It is of great value, whether praying privately, as a family, or in the church. Dionysius Bar Salibi (d.1171), the great Syriac scholar and saint, writes, "This book [Shehimo] was prepared for chanting by the simple worshippers and monastics. This is why its compilers chose simple verses which would immediately be assimilated by the mind and would move the heart". The following suggestions may help you incorporate the Shehimo into your daily life:

1. Dedicate a room, wall, or space (on the eastern side) in your home or room that is set apart for prayer;
2. Place a Bible, icon, and candle in that dedicated place to help you maintain focus and attention during prayer.
3. When it is physically possible, pray the Shehimo standing up and facing towards the east.
4. Prostrate and kneel before God during the Trisagion, Praise of the Cherubim, and the Nicene Creed.
5. Know that certain prayers and psalms are fixed daily prayers, which are common to each office of each day. These prayers and psalms are found in the opening part of the Shehimo called the "Common".

6. In addition to the Common, each office of each day has unique prayers that differ from each other.

7. Each office begins with a Qaumo followed by an Introductory Prayer. Each office concludes with a Qaumo and the Nicene Creed (if it is the terminal office prayed at that time).

8. The Quqlion or Intercessory Prayers are offered at the conclusion of the evening and morning times of prayer (at the conclusion of Sapro and Ramsho).

9. Specific directions have been included in the Shehimo to help you navigate between the Common and the specific Office of the day.

10. If praying the entire office or all the offices of the day is too overwhelming, try to incorporate a little into your prayer life at a time. Begin with the prayers and psalms of the Common and slowly grow your discipline of prayer according to your time and situation in life. The more time we set apart for God the greater we can develop our relationship with Him.

About the Versification

We give glory to God for the efforts of Father Bede Griffiths of the Kurishmala Ashram, whose wonderful English translation of the Syriac Shehimo is the basis of this current versification. We also give thanks to God for the efforts of all His servants who have spent countless hours over the past eight years versifying the Shehimo. They have attempted to adhere to the rich theological witnesss and musicality of the Syriac liturgical tradition in a meaningful and clear way in the English language. Finally, we pray above all, that the Shehimo become a useful and vital part of the everyday life of the worshipping English-speaking faithful of the Church.

Metropolitan Alexios Eusebius
Feast of Epiphany, 2016

PREFATORY PRAYER

We pray standing upright while facing East as we collect our thoughts on God.

† In the name of the Father, and of the Son, and of the Holy Spirit, one true God;

Glory be to Him, and may His grace and mercy be upon us forever. Amin.

Holy, Holy, Holy, Lord God Almighty, by whose glory, the heaven and earth are filled. Hosanna in the Highest!

Blessed is He, who has come,/ and is to come, in the name of the Lord; Glory be to Him in the Highest!

QAUMO

Each Hour of Prayer BEGINS and CONCLUDES with a Qaumo, except when the Praise of the Cherubim is prayed at the conclusion of Compline.

We make the sign of the Cross and kneel as we pray "Crucified for us…"

Holy art Thou, O God!
Holy art Thou, Almighty!
Holy art Thou, Immortal!
+ Crucified for us, Have mercy upon us! *(Three times)*

Lord, have mercy upon us!
Lord, be kind and have mercy!
Lord, accept our service and our prayers!
Have mercy upon us!

Glory be to Thee, O God!
Glory be to Thee, O Creator!
Glory be to Thee, O Christ the King
Who has compassion on His sinful servants. Barekmor

Our Father, who art in heaven, Hallowed be Thy name. Thy kingdom come, Thy will be done on earth as it is in heaven. Give us this day, our daily bread and forgive us our debts and sins as we also have forgiven our debtors. Lead us not into temptation, but deliver us from the evil one. +For Thine is the kingdom, the power and the glory, forever and ever. Amin.

(This prayer is not originally part of the Qaumo, but may be recited.)

Peace be with You, Mary, full of grace, / our Lord is with you. Blessed are you among women,/ and blessed is the fruit of your womb, our Lord Jesus, Christ./ O, Virgin Saint Mary, Mother of God,/ pray for us sinners, / now and at all times, and at the hour of our death. Amin.

Go to the Hour of Prayer:

NICENE CREED

The Nicene Creed is prayed at the conclusion of the Hour. We make the sign of the cross and kneel three times when we recall Christ's Incarnation, Crucifixion, and Resurrection.

We believe in one true God, the Father Almighty / Maker of heaven and earth / and of all things visible and invisible.

And in One Lord Jesus Christ / the Only-Begotten Son of God / begotten of the Father before all worlds / Light of Light / True God of True God / begotten,/ not made / being of one essence with the Father / and by Whom all things were made; / Who for us men and for our salvation / came down from heaven

+ And was incarnate of the Holy Spirit / and of the Holy Virgin Mary, Mother of God/and became man,

+ And was crucified for us / in the days of Pontius Pilate / and suffered, and died, and was buried,

+ And on the third day rose again/ according to His Will / and ascended into heaven / and sits at the right hand of His Father / and shall come again in His great glory / to judge both the living and the dead / whose kingdom shall have no end.

And in the one Living Holy Spirit / the life-giving Lord of all / Who proceeds from the Father / and Who together with the Father and the Son / is worshipped and glorified/ who spoke through the prophets and the apostles.

And in the One, Holy, Catholic and Apostolic Church./ And we confess one baptism for the remission of sins / and look for the resurrection of the dead /and the new life in the world to come. Amin.

Lord have mercy, Lord have mercy, Lord have mercy,
(Kurielaison, Kurielaison, Kurielaison)

Lord, have mercy upon us,
Lord, be kind and have mercy,
Answer Lord, and have mercy.

Glory be to You, O Lord,
Glory be to You, O Lord,
Glory be to You, our hope forever. Barekmor.

COMMON of VESPERS **[RAMSHO]**

Introductory Prayer

† Glory be to the Father and to the Son and to the Holy Spirit.

May His grace and mercy be upon us, weak and sinful, in both worlds forever and ever. Amin

Grant us, Lord God, that while our bodies rest from the labors of the day and our souls are released from worldly thoughts, we may stand in Your presence with tranquility at this time of evening and that we may offer You ceaseless praise and uninterrupted thanksgiving; that we may acknowledge Your loving kindness by which You direct and rule our lives and protect and save our souls; to You we offer praise and thanksgiving, now and always, forever and ever, Amin.

Psalms of Vespers

[Psalm 141] **Kurielaison / Lord, I have called upon You, / answer me; hear and receive my words.**

Let my prayer be like incense in Your sight, / the offering of my hands like the evening offering. / Set a guard, Lord, before my mouth, /a guard before my lips, / that my heart may not turn to evil words /and I may not do deeds of wickedness.

Let me not take salt with impious men; / let the just man teach me and reprove me: / let not the oil of the impious anoint my head; / because my prayer was against their evil-doing: / their judges have been restrained by the side of the rock; / and they have heard how gentle are my words.

As when a plough cleaves the earth their bones have been scattered at the mouth of Sheol. / I have lifted up my eyes to You, Lord, / and in You have I put my trust, /do not cast away my soul.

Keep me from the hand of the proud, who have laid snares for me; / let the wicked fall into their nets, while I pass on.

[Psalm 142] With my voice I cried to the Lord; / with my voice I besought the Lord and poured out my prayer before him; / I showed him my affliction when my spirit was troubled, / but You know my path.

In the way of my walking they have laid a snare for me; / I look to the right and see none that knows me; / the way of escape has gone from me and there is none who cares for my soul. / I cried to You, Lord, and said: / You are my hope and my portion in the land of the living.

Hear my petition because I am brought very low; / deliver me from my persecutors because they are too strong for me. / Lead me forth from prison that I may give thanks to Your name: / Your just ones shall have hope when You shall reward me.

[Psalm 119, 105-112] **Your word is a lamp to my feet and light to my path; / I have sworn and am resolved to keep the judgments of Your justice. / I am greatly brought low, Lord, / give me life according to Your word; / be pleased with the words of my mouth, Lord, / and teach me Your judgments.**

My soul is ever in my hands, and I have not forgotten Your law; / sinners have laid snares for me and I have not strayed from Your commands. / I shall inherit Your testimony forever because it is dear to my heart; / I have turned my heart to do Your commands forever in truth.

[Psalm 117] **Praise the Lord, all you nations; praise him, all you peoples; / for His grace is strong over us, / truly the Lord is forever.**

And to You belongs the praise, O God. Barekmor.

† ***Glory to the Father, Son, and Holy Spirit.***
Unto the ages of ages and forevermore.

Turn to the Vespers of the Day
Q–p.28; Mon–p.58 Tue–p.80 Wed– p.103 Thu–p.128 Fri–p.151 Sat–p.176

Concluding Prayer

O Lord Jesus Christ, do not close the door of Your mercy in our faces.
We confess that we are sinners, have mercy upon us. / O Lord, Your love made you descend to us from Your place, / that by Your death our death might be abolished. / Have mercy upon us. Amin.

Qaumo (p. 5)

COMMON of COMPLINE [SOUTORO]

Introductory Prayer

† Glory be to the Father and to the Son and to the Holy Spirit.

May His grace and mercy be upon us, weak and sinful, in both worlds forever and ever. Amin

Protect us, Lord, beneath the wings of Your loving kindness and turn our hard hearts to the knowledge of Your truth; grant us to know and to consider that the evening which has called us to rest and refreshment from labor is a figure of the end of this present life; that we may be diligent in good actions which are pleasing to Your will, and we will offer You praise and thanksgiving, O Father, Son and Holy Spirit; now and always, forever and ever. Amin.

Turn to the Compline of the Day
Q–p.34; Mon–p.63 Tue–p.85 Wed– p.108 Thu–p.133 Fri–p.156 Sat–p.181

Psalms of Compline

[Psalm 91] **Barekmor. / He who sits under the protection of the Most High / and glories in the shelter of God will say to the Lord,**

"My trust is in You, / God is my refuge in whom I trust".

For the Lord shall deliver you from the snare, which makes you stumble / and from talk of vain things.

He will keep you safe under his feathers / and you shall be protected beneath His wings. / His truth shall enclose you as an armor.

You shall not be afraid of the terror of the night / nor of the arrow, which flies by day.

Nor of the word, which walks in the darkness / nor of the spirit that destroys at midday.

Thousands shall fall at your side / and ten thousand at your right hand, / but it shall not come near you

But with your eyes alone / you shall see the reward of the wicked

Because You have made the Lord your trust; / You have made Your dwelling in the heights

Evil shall not come near you, / affliction shall not come near your tent

Because He has commanded his angels concerning you; / that they should keep you in all your ways

And receive you in their arms; / that you may not stumble with your foot

You shall tread upon the adder and the basilisk; / You shall trample upon the lion and the dragon

"Because he has cried to me", says the Lord, / "I will deliver him and strengthen him."

Because he has known my name, He shall call upon me and I will answer him, / I will be with him in distress.

I will strengthen him and honor him; / I will satisfy Him with length of days and show him my salvation".

[Psalm 121] **I have lifted up my eyes to the hills - from where will my help come?**

My help is from the Lord, / who made heaven and earth

He will not suffer your foot to slip, / your guardian shall not sleep.

Indeed, He neither slumbers nor sleeps, / the guardian of Israel.

The Lord is your guardian. / The Lord shall shelter you with His right hand

The sun shall not harm you by day, / nor the moon by night,

The Lord shall guard your going out and your coming in. / From henceforth and forevermore.

And to You belongs the praise, O God. Barekmor.

+ Glory be to the Father and to the Son and to the Holy Spirit.

Halleluiah, Halleluiah, Halleluiah. Unto the ages of ages and forevermore.

Prayer of Mor Severus

He who sits under the protection of the Most High, / beneath the shadow of the wings of Your loving kindness will say,

"Protect us, O Lord, and have mercy upon us; / You who hear all, / hear the prayer of Your servants in Your loving kindness.

Grant us, O Christ our Savior, / an evening full of peace and a night of holiness, / for You are the King of Glory.

Our eyes are turned to You. / Pardon our offences and our sins; / Have mercy upon us / both in this world and in the world to come;

O Lord, may Your mercy protect us / and Your grace rest upon our faces. / May Your + Cross guard us from the evil one and his powers.

May your right hand rest upon us all the days of our lives, / and Your peace reign among us. /Give hope and salvation to the souls of those who pray to You.

By the prayer of Mary, who bore You and of all Your saints, / pardon us and have mercy on us, O God". Amin.

Praise of the Cherubim

We make the sign of the Cross and kneel as we pray, "Blessed is the glory…"

† Blessed is the glory of the Lord, from His place forever!

† Blessed is the glory of the Lord, from His place forever!

† Blessed is the glory of the Lord, from His place forever and ever!

Holy and glorious Trinity, have mercy upon us;

Holy and glorious Trinity, have mercy upon us;

Holy and glorious Trinity, have compassion and mercy upon us.

You are holy and glorious forever

You are holy and glorious forever

You are holy and blessed is Your name, forever and ever.

Glory be to You, O Lord.

Glory be to You, O Lord;

Glory be to You, our hope forever. Barekmor.

Our Father who art in Heaven (p. 5)

COMMON of NIGHT VIGIL [LILIO]

Introductory Prayer

† Glory be to the Father and to the Son and to the Holy Spirit.

May His grace and mercy be upon us, weak and sinful, in both worlds forever and ever. Amin

Awaken us, Lord, from our sleep in the sloth of sin that we may praise your watchfulness, You who watch and do not sleep; give life to our death in the sleep of death and corruption, that we may adore Your compassion, You who live and do not die; grant us in the glorious company of the angels who praise You in heaven, to praise You and bless you in holiness, because You are praised and blessed in heaven and on earth, Father, Son and Holy Spirit, now and always and forever. Amin.

Introductory Psalms of Night Vigil

[Psalm 134] **Barekmor. Bless the Lord, / all You servants of the Lord.**

Barekmor. You who stand by night in the house of the Lord.

Lift up your hands to the holy place / and bless the Lord.

May the Lord bless you from Zion, / He who made heaven and earth.

[Psalm 119, 169-176] **Let my praise enter before You, Lord, / and give me life by Your word; / let my cry enter before You, Lord, / and deliver me by Your word.**

My tongue shall pour forth Your word, / because all Your commands are just.

My lips shall speak Your praise when You have taught me Your commands; / let Your hand help me / because I have taken pleasure in Your commands.

My soul has longed for Your salvation /and I have meditated on Your law; / let my soul live and I will praise You /and Your judgments shall help me.

I have gone astray like a lost sheep; / seek for Your servant, / because I have not forgotten all Your commands.

[Psalm 117] Praise the Lord, all you nations, /praise Him, all you peoples; / because His grace is strong over us, / the Lord is truly forever. *And to You belongs the praise, O God.*

† Glory to the Father, Son, and Holy Spirit.

Unto the ages of ages and forevermore.

Turn to the Eniyono of Night Vigil for the Day
***Q**–p.35; **Mon**–p.65 **Tue**–p.87 **Wed**– p.110 **Thu**–p.134 **Fri**–p.157 **Sat**–p.182*

1st *Qaumo Introductory Prayer*

To the honor and glory of Your loving kindness may we stand before Your Majesty, Lord God, and may we call to mind by night and by day, Worshipful and Holy One, Your divine commands, that with David the Psalmist we may cry and say, "In the middle of the night, I arose to give thanks for Your judgments with regard to us, so fair and far beyond understanding, our Lord and our God, forever!" Amin.

Turn to the 1st Qaumo of the Night Vigil for the Day
***Q**–p.36; **Mon**–p.65 **Tue**–p.87 **Wed**– p.110 **Thu**–p.135 **Fri**–p.158 or p. 160*
***Sat**–p.183*

Praise of the Cherubim

Prayed at the conclusion of the 1st and 2nd Qaume of Night Vigil

† Blessed is the glory of the Lord, from His place forever!
† Blessed is the glory of the Lord, from His place forever!
† Blessed is the glory of the Lord, from His place forever and ever!

Holy and glorious Trinity, have mercy upon us;
Holy and glorious Trinity, have mercy upon us;
Holy and glorious Trinity, have compassion and mercy upon us.

You are holy and glorious forever
You are holy and glorious forever
You are holy and blessed is Your name, forever and ever.

Glory be to You, O Lord.
Glory be to You, O Lord;
Glory be to You, our hope forever. Barekmor.

Our Father who art in Heaven (p. 5)

2nd Qaumo Introductory Prayer

Mingle, Lord, by Your grace, our songs with the songs of the angels without flesh above this world, that with one accord, with the voice of the Spirit, we may cry and say, "Blessed be the glory of the Lord in His place forever and ever!" Amin.

Turn to the 2nd Qaumo of the Night Vigil for the Day

***Q*–p.37; *Mon*–p.67 *Tue*–p.89 *Wed*– p.112 *Thu*–p.137 *Fri*–p.161 *Sat*–p.184**

Praise of the Cherubim

Prayed at the conclusion of the 1st and 2nd Qaume of Night Vigil

† Blessed is the glory of the Lord, from His place forever!
† Blessed is the glory of the Lord, from His place forever!
† Blessed is the glory of the Lord, from His place forever and ever!

Holy and glorious Trinity, have mercy upon us;
Holy and glorious Trinity, have mercy upon us;
Holy and glorious Trinity, have compassion and mercy upon us.

You are holy and glorious forever
You are holy and glorious forever
You are holy and blessed is Your name, forever and ever.

Glory be to You, O Lord.
Glory be to You, O Lord;
Glory be to You, our hope forever. Barekmor.

Our Father who art in Heaven (p. 5)

3rd Qaumo Introductory Prayer

Sincere and grateful praises with sweet and pleasant voices does the Church with her children raise to the Father, the Son, and the Holy Spirit at all times together with the four-winged Cherubim and the six-winged Seraphim and with the angels who cry and say, "Blessed is the glory of the Lord in His place forever and ever!" Amin.

Turn to the 3rd Qaumo of the Night Vigil for the Day

***Q*–p.38; *Mon*–p.68 *Tue*–p.90 *Wed*– p.114 *Thu*–p.139 *Fri*–p.163 *Sat*–p.186**

Following the 3rd Qaumo of Night Vigil

† Halleluiah, halleluiah, halleluiah! Glory to You, O God! (3x)

Be compassionate towards us in Your mercy, / O God of compassion; / in our sacrifices and our prayers / we make memory of our fathers /who taught us while they were alive, / to be children of God; / O Son of God, / raise them up in the heavenly kingdom / with the just and the righteous / in the world, which does not pass away.

Song of Mary

Mary said, "My soul magnifies the Lord, and my spirit rejoices in God my Savior / because He has looked upon the lowliness of His handmaid; / for behold, from henceforth all generations shall call me blessed.

Because He who is mighty has done great things for me and holy is His name. / And His mercy is from generation to generation on those who fear Him.

He has won victory with His arm, He has scattered the proud in the conceit of their heart. / He has put down the mighty from their thrones, and has exalted the lowly.

He has filled the hungry with good things and the rich He has sent away empty. / He has given help to Israel, His servant, mindful of His mercy / even as he spoke to our fathers, to Abraham and his seed forever...*Barekmor*

† Glory to the Father, Son, and Holy Spirit.
Unto the ages of ages and forevermore. Amin

Turn to the Mawrbo of the Night Vigil for the Day (p. 199)

[Psalm 133] **How good and fair it is for brethren to dwell together in unity.**

Like the oil which descends upon the head and upon the beard. / Even the beard of Aaron, and descends to the hem of his robe. / Like the dew of Hermon, which descends on the mountain of Zion.

Because there the Lord promised a blessing and life forevermore.

And to You belongs the praise, O God. Barekmor

† Glory to the Father, Son, and Holy Spirit.
Unto the ages of ages and forevermore.

Eniyono

Let us make memory of Mary and may she help us by her prayers.

Let us make memory of the just and may they help us by their prayers.

Prophets, apostles and martyrs, may your prayer be a stronghold to us.

Make us worthy, Lord, of the harbour of Your martyrs and of the dwelling of your friends.

Compassionate and full of mercy, on the day of Your judgment, have mercy on us.

Blessed is He who does not keep His mercy from the sinner who calls upon Him. Barekmor.

† Glory to the Father, Son, and Holy Spirit. Make a good memory, Lord, of the children of the Faithful Church.

Unto the ages of ages and forevermore. And let them stand at Your right hand on the day when Your Majesty appears.

Alternate Eniyono

At all times and at all seasons, virgin Mother of God / may your prayer be a stronghold for us.

By the prayers of Your saints / keep from us the evil one who at all times lays snares for us.

Jesus, our Lord, and our God, / may Your Cross be a stronghold for us and may we be protected beneath it.

Jesus, Word of God, / guard the living by Your Cross and pardon the dead in Your mercy.

On all the days of our life / let us thank and worship and praise the Father, the Son and the Holy Spirit.

Our God, full of mercy, on the great day when You come, / raise us up at Your right hand.

You who have made us worthy to sing praise to You at this time / make us worthy to inherit Your kingdom.

May Your mercy be upon us, Lord, / Lord of our death and our life, / have mercy on our souls.

Lord, have mercy upon us and help us.

Psalms of Night Vigil

Awake, you that sleep, and rise and sing praise. ***[Psalm 148]*** **Praise the Lord from the heavens, praise Him in the heights.**

Praise Him, all His angels; praise Him, all his hosts.

Praise Him, sun and moon; praise Him, all stars of light; praise Him, heaven of heavens, and the waters above the heavens: let them praise the name of the Lord.

For He spoke and they were made, He commanded and they were created; He established them forever and ever, He gave them a law, which shall not pass away.

Praise the Lord from the earth, sea-monsters and all depths; fire and hail, snow and mist, stormy winds that fulfill His word.

Mountains and all hills, fruit trees and all cedars; wild beasts and all cattle, creeping things and birds that fly.

Kings of the earth and all peoples, princes and all judges of the earth: young men too and maidens, old men and boys: let them praise the name of the Lord.

For His name alone is exalted; His praise is on earth and in heaven, and He has lifted up the horn of His people; praise for all the just, the children of Israel, the people who draw near to Him.

[Psalm 149] **Praise the Lord with a new praise in the assembly of the just; let Israel be glad in her Maker, let the children of Zion rejoice in their King.**

Let them praise His name with the timbrel and the drum, let them sing to Him with the harp: for the Lord takes pleasure in His people, and gives salvation to the poor.

Let the just exult in glory, let them praise Him on their beds: let the high praises of God be in their throats, and two-edged swords in their hands.

To execute vengeance on the nations, and to rebuke the peoples; to bind their kings with chains, their nobles with fetters of iron, to execute on them the judgment which is written: that is the glory of the just.

[Psalm 150] **Praise the Lord in His holy place, praise Him in the firmament of His strength.**

Praise Him for His mighty deeds, praise Him for His abounding greatness, praise Him with the sound of the trumpet, praise Him with lyre and harp.

Praise Him with the timbrel and the drum, praise Him with the soft strings, praise Him with the loud cymbals; praise Him with the sound of the voice; let everything that has breath praise the Lord.

[Psalm 117] Praise the Lord, all you nations; praise Him, all you peoples. For His grace is strong over us, truly the Lord is forever.

And to you belongs the praise, O God. Barekmor.

† Glory to the Father, Son, and Holy Spirit.
Unto the ages of ages and forevermore.

Praise to the Holy Trinity!
Praise to the Holy Trinity!
We praise the glorious Trinity, self-existent and eternal; and to You belongs the praise, O God, at all times.

If Qyomtho, turn to p. 40, otherwise continue onwards.

INTERCESSORY PRAYER OF NIGHT VIGIL – QUQLION

Pethgomo

The righteous shall flourish like a palm tree. Halleluiah
Like cedars of Lebanon – they shall grow.

They shall flourish and be great in old age. Halleluiah
They shall be fruitful – and fragrant…Barekmor.

† Glory be to the Father, Son and the Holy Spirit.
Unto to the ages of ages and forever more.

Eqbo

Your mem'ry O St. (Thomas)
be kept here and in Heaven
May your pray'r be a help to
Those who honor your mem'ry. *Stoumen kalos, Kurielaison*

Turn to the Qole of the Night Vigil for the Day
Q*–p.40;* ***Mon****–p.70* ***Tue****–p.92* ***Wed****– p.115* ***Thu****–p.140* ***Fri****–p.164* ***Sat****–p.187*

Hymn of the Angels

As the angels and archangels on high in heaven sing praise, / so we poor children of earth sing praise and say:

At all times and at all seasons, Glory to God in the heights / and on earth, peace and tranquility and good hope for the sons of men.

We praise You, we bless You, we worship You, / we raise up a hymn of praise to You.

We give thanks to You because of Your great glory, / Lord our creator, king of heaven, / God the Father Almighty.

Lord God, only Son, Jesus Christ, with the Holy Spirit,

Lord God, Lamb of God, Son and Word of the Father, / who take away, or rather have taken away, the sin of the world / have mercy upon us.

You who take away, or rather have taken away the sin of the world, / incline Your ear to us and receive our prayers; / You who sit in glory at the right hand of the Father, / have compassion on us.

Because You only are holy, You only, Lord Jesus Christ, / with the Holy Spirit, in the glory of God the Father. Amin.

At all times and all the days of my life, / I will bless and praise Your name, which is holy and blessed forever, / and which remains forever and ever.

Blessed are You, Lord Almighty, God of our fathers, / and Your name is blessed and glorified in praise forever.

To You belongs glory, to You belongs praise, to You belongs honor, / God of all, Father of truth, / with the only Son and living Holy Spirit, now and always, forever and ever. Amin.

Concluding Prayer

O Lord Jesus Christ, do not close the door of Your mercy in our faces. We confess that we are sinners, have mercy upon us. / O Lord, Your love made you descend to us from Your place, / that by Your death our death might be abolished. / Have mercy upon us. Amin.

Qaumo (p. 5)

COMMON of MATINS [SAPRO]

Introductory Prayer

† Glory be to the Father and to the Son and to the Holy Spirit.

May His grace and mercy be upon us, weak and sinful, in both worlds forever and ever. Amin

Creator of the morning, who drives out the darkness and brings light and joy to the creation, create in us habits of virtue and drive from us all the darkness of sin; give us light and joy by the glorious rays of Your grace, our Lord and our God, forever. Amin.

Psalms of Matins

[Psalm 51] **Have mercy upon me, O God, in Your loving kindness; / in the abundance of Your mercy blot out my sin.**

Wash me thoroughly from my guilt and cleanse me from my sin./ For I acknowledge my fault and my sins are before me always.

Against you only have I sinned and done evil in Your sight, / that You may be justified in Your words and vindicated in Your judgment. / For I was born in guilt and in sin did my mother conceive me.

But you take pleasure in truth and You have made known to me the secrets of Your wisdom. / Sprinkle me with Your hyssop and I shall be clean; / wash me and I shall be whiter than snow.

Give me the comfort of Your joy and gladness, and the bones, which have been humbled shall rejoice. / Turn away Your face from my sins and blot out all my faults.

Create in me a clean heart, O God, / and renew Your steadfast spirit within me. / Do not cast me from Your presence / and take not Your Holy Spirit from me.

But restore to me Your joy and Your salvation / and let Your glorious spirit sustain me; / that I may teach the wicked Your way / and sinners may return to You.

Deliver me from blood, O God, God of my salvation / and my tongue shall praise Your justice. / Lord, open my lips and my mouth shall sing Your praise.

For you do not take pleasure in sacrifices; / by burnt offerings You are not appeased. / The sacrifice of God is a humble spirit, / a heart that is contrite God will not despise.

Do good in Your good pleasure to Zion and build up the walls of Jerusalem. / Then shall You be satisfied with sacrifices of truth and with whole burnt-offerings; / then shall they offer bullocks upon Your altar.

And to You belongs the praise, O God. Barekmor.

(If Qyomtho, turn to p.43, otherwise continue to next Psalm)

† Glory be to the Father and to the Son and to the Holy Spirit.

Unto the ages of ages and forevermore.

O Merciful God! Have mercy upon us in your mercy!

Lord have mercy upon us and help us.

[Psalm 63] **My God, you are my God, I will seek You.**

My soul thirsts for You and my flesh seeks for You like the thirsty earth, which is parched and begging for water.

So have I looked for You in truth, that I may see Your power and Your glory.

Because your loving-kindness is better than life, / my lips shall praise You.

So I will bless You while I live and will lift up my hands in Your name.

My soul shall be enriched as with marrow and fat / and my mouth shall praise You with lips of praise.

I have remembered You upon my bed / and in the nighttime I have meditated on You.

For You have been my helper / and in the shadow of Your wings is my protection.

My soul follows after You / and Your right hand upholds me.

Those who seek to destroy my soul shall enter into the lower parts of the earth.

They shall be delivered over to the sword and shall be food for foxes; / but the king shall rejoice in God.

Everyone who swears by Him shall glory, / but the mouth of those who speak lies shall be stopped.

And to You belongs the praise, O God. Barekmor.

† Glory to the Father, Son, and Holy Spirit.
Unto the ages of ages and forevermore.

Turn to the Eniyono of Matins of the Day
***Q**–p.44; **Mon**–p.71 **Tue**–p.93 **Wed**– p.117 **Thu**–p.141 **Fri**–p.165 **Sat**–p.189*

[Psalm 113] **Amin. Praise you servants of the Lord, praise the name of the Lord.**

May the Lord's name be bless'd forever and ever.

From the rising of the sun to its setting / great is the name of the Lord.

The Lord is high above all peoples / and his glory is above the heavens.

Who is like the Lord, our God, who sits on high / and looks upon the depths in heaven and on earth?

He raises up the poor from the dunghill / and makes him sit with the princes of the people.

He makes the barren woman keep house / and be a joyful mother of children.

And to You belongs the praise, O God. Barekmor.

† Glory to the Father, Son, and Holy Spirit.
Unto the ages of ages and forevermore.

Turn to Eqbo of the Day
***Q**–p.48; **Mon**–p.72 **Tue**–p.93 **Wed**– p.117 **Thu**–p.142 **Fri**–p.166 **Sat**–p.189*

Concluding Prayer

It is good to give thanks to the Lord and to sing praise to Your name, Most High; / to proclaim Your grace in the morning and Your faithfulness in the night. / Lord, in the morning You shall hear my voice / and in the morning I have prepared myself to appear before You. / Lord, have compassion on Your people; / Lord, pardon and forgive the sins of all of us. / Holy One, let Your right hand rest upon us and pardon our infirmity / because Your name is forever. Amin.

Qaumo (p. 5)

COMMON of THIRD HOUR

Introductory Prayer

† Glory be to the Father and to the Son and to the Holy Spirit.

May His grace and mercy be upon us, weak and sinful, in both worlds forever and ever. Amin

Cleanse us, Lord, by repentance and by tears of compunction from every passion and stain and defilement of sin, and grant us the grace of victory in our lives at all times and for all the days of our life, O Father, Son and Holy Spirit, now and always, forever and ever. Amin.

Turn to the Third Hour of the Day

***Qyomtho**–p.54;*

***Monday** –p.77*

***Tuesday**–p.100*

***Wednesday**– p.124*

***Thursday**–p.148*

***Friday**–p.173*

***Saturday**–p.196*

COMMON of SIXTH HOUR

Introductory Prayer

† Glory be to the Father and to the Son and to the Holy Spirit.

May His grace and mercy be upon us, weak and sinful, in both worlds forever and ever. Amin

Enlighten, Lord, the eyes of our minds by the light of Your glory, that while we walk in it we may turn aside from the paths and snares of the enemy. Strengthen our hearts in Your commandments and our hands in the doing of good. Direct, Lord God, our walking according to Your word and our thoughts to meditation on You; keep our lips and our tongues by Your help for the voice of Your praise; establish the truth of Your teaching in us and deliver us from every kind of sin, for in You is our hope and on You we call, our Lord and our God, forever. Amin.

Turn to the Sixth Hour of the Day

Qyomtho–*p.55;*

Monday –*p.78*

Tuesday–*p.101*

Wednesday– *p.126*

Thursday–*p.149*

Friday–*p.174*

Saturday–*p.197*

BO'UTHO of MOR BALAI

Lord, by the pray'r of Your mother and saints,
Have mercy on us and our departed.

May Mary's mem'ry be for our blessing,
And may her pray'r be a refuge for us.

Prophets, Apostles, and holy Martyrs,
Beseech and beg for mercy for us all.

Sprinkle the dew of gladness on the heads
Of our departed who sleep in Your hope.

Praise to Him who has honored His mother,
Glorified the saints, and raised up the dead.

Lord, by the pray'r of Your mother and saints,
Have mercy on us and our departed.

MANITHO *of* MOR SEVERUS

By the prayers of Your Mother – and those of all Your Saints

I exalt You, Lord and King, - The Only-Begotten Son;
Word of the Father;
Immortal in His nature and who by His grace
Descended for – all mankind
To bring life and salvation for our fallen human race;
Who did become – incarnate – of the pure Virgin,
The holy and glor`i`ous The`o`tokos
He became man – without change
And was crucified for us, Christ who is our Lord and God.
He trampled death – by His death - and destroyed our death.
Christ, who is one of the Holy Trinity;
Who is worshipped – equally
With His Father and Spirit; Have mercy upon us all!

Qaumo (p. 5)

COMMON OF NINTH HOUR

Introductory Prayer

† Glory be to the Father and to the Son and to the Holy Spirit.

May His grace and mercy be upon us, weak and sinful, in both worlds forever and ever. Amin

Receive, Lord, the souls of Your servants in tabernacles of light and make them to dwell in the harbor of blessedness; give them rest in the glorious bosom of the Patriarchs: Abraham, Isaac, and Jacob, that on the great day of Your glorious manifestation, we may stand with them at Your right hand, and offer fitting praise to You and to Your Father and to Your Holy Spirit, now and always, forever and ever, Amin.

Turn to the Ninth Hour of the Day
***Q**–p.57; **Mon**–p.79 **Tue**–p.102 **Wed**–p.127 **Thu**–p.150 **Fri**–p.175 **Sat**–p.198*

BO'UTHO of MOR BALAI

Renew Your creatures by the res'rrection,
Your worshippers who have slept in Your hope.

Give rest and pardon to the dead, O Lord,
Who sleep in hope and await Your coming.

Lord, with Abraham, Isaac and Jacob,
Make Your servants rest, those who sleep in hope.

Their bodies and souls shall cry together:
"Bless'd is He who will come and raise th e dead."

OR

O Merciful Lord, renew Your creation at the Resurrection. / Absolve and grant rest to those in the grave, / Your servants and worshippers, who have slept in Your hope and await Your coming. / O Heavenly King, / multiply forgiveness to the faithful departed / and make them dwell in the bosom of Abraham, Isaac, and Jacob. / Glory to Christ who calls the dead and they rise without corruption and sing praise. / Their bodies and souls shall cry together: / "Blessed is He who has come and is to come / and will raise the dead." Amin.

Qaumo (p. 5)

VESPERS of QYOMTHO [Sunday]

Qaumo (p. 5)

Introductory Prayer of Qyomtho

† Glory be to the Father and to the Son and to the Holy Spirit.

May His grace and mercy be upon us, weak and sinful, in both worlds forever and ever. Amin.

Grant us, Lord God, that with the heavenly hosts we may exalt this day of Your Resurrection on the third day in purity and holiness, that we may shine before You in virtuous conduct and may praise You without ceasing, with Your Father and Your Holy Spirit, now and always, forever and ever. Amin.

Turn to ***Psalm 51 (p. 21)***

ENIYONO

(Htith Lokh/Ee ninudhanathil…)

Adam - the head of our race will rejoice at
The Resurrection
O Lord - have mercy upon us all!

They placed - You in a tomb sealed with stone and guard
After You had died
O Lord - have mercy upon us all!

The Christ - by His resurrection gladdened all
In heaven and earth
O Lord - have mercy upon us all!

The myrrh - bearing women set out for Your tomb
With fragrant perfumes
O Lord - have mercy upon us all!

John and - Simon ran to the tomb of the Lord
and reached there with joy
O Lord - have mercy upon us all! *Barekmor*

+ Glory be to the Father, Son and Holy Spirit
Unto the ages of ages and for ever more.

Glory -to Your mercy and praise to Your grace
O God our Savior
O Lord - have mercy upon us all!

Turn to ***Psalms of Vespers (p. 8)***

ENIYONO

(Sli b'Moriyo b'Rahme/En naadha nin krupa ninne…)

By Your grace, You were inclined
To descend to us sinners
By Your grace, pity Your Church
Which clings to the wings *of Your* Cross

Christ, who rose up from the dead
In pow`er and great glory
By your mercy, raise us from
The abyss of our foul deeds

On this noble, holy day
Of Your Resurrection, Lord
Grant remission of our debts
So that we may praise Your grace

Cherubim guarded Eden
In which the tree of life grew
And Watchers guarded the tomb
From which Christ the King came forth

Churches and monasteries
Sing praise, rejoice, and glory
In the resurrection of
Christ the King upon this day. *Barekmor.*

+ Glory be to the Father, Son and Holy Spirit
Unto the ages of ages and forevermore.

Christ, by Your Resurrection
You gladdened the departed
By it, gladden us, O Lord
And raise us to Your right hand…*Staumen Kalos. Kurielaison*

(Promion & Sedro is read)

QOLO

(Lokh Moriyo Qorenan/Naadhan mrutharidayil urappi chaadathe…)

In the house of death, our Lord consoled Adam:
"Do not grieve that you had transgressed the commandment
For the sins and offenses you committed
I was beaten in order to save you from death
You wore leaves – for you were naked
Naked they - hung me on the tree
And the Father was pleased by the blood, which I shed. *Barekmor*

+ Glory be to the Father, Son and Holy Spirit

O Holy Church, rejoice for Christ is Risen
He resurrected from the tomb on - the third day
By His death, He trampled death ending our death
By the lance which pierced Him, He turned the - Cherub's lance
He dissolved - the tomb's corruption
He gave life - through resurrection
He endured all these things and saved us from error

Unto the ages of ages and forevermore.

Let us beseech Christ for all the departed
Who ate His Body and drank His life-giving Blood
That the darkness of sin not reign over them,
Over their souls and their spirits in - the Kingdom
Lord receive - the spirits of those
Who confessed - You and Your Passion
Call to them and raise them up at Your right hand side

Lord have mercy upon us and help us.

(Etro is read)

QOLO

(Quqoyo/Nin murivukaleeten mooron manamen naadha…)

The scent of Chrism, O Lord, rises from Your wounds
Your lips are like the threads of the finest scarlet *(Sol 4:3)*
I sought You and - guards surrounded me
From them I ran - unto Golgotha
There I saw Your side pierced and Your blood flowing out
Astonished I cried, "Glory - to You for You have
Halleluiah - saved us by Your Cross". *Barekmor*

+ *Glory be to the Father, Son and Holy Spirit*

Your beauty, O Son of God, has enchanted me
How shall I ever find the words to sing to You?
On high You sit - at the Father's right
In the depths You - were between two thieves
Your grave is laid in She`ol - Your throne in heaven
In the heights and depths, the men and Watchers cry out:
Halleluiah - "Glory to You Lord!"

Unto the ages of ages and forevermore.

Lord, remember and grant rest to our departed
Who put You on in baptism and received You
    From the altar - they ate Your Body
    And drank from the - cup of salvation
May they rejoice in the Kingdom with Abraham
And at Your right hand may they cry, "Glory to You".
        Halleluiah - Grant them rest, O Lord!

GOSPEL of VESPERS

Halleluiah, Halleluiah
Let the heavens rejoice and let the earth be glad
At the resurrection of Christ the King
Halleluiah

Deacon: Barekmor. With stillness, fear and purity, let us attend and listen to the Good News of the living words of God, in the Holy Gospel of our Lord Jesus Christ, that is read to us.

Priest: + Peace be unto you all.

People: Make us worthy, O Lord God, with Thy Spirit.

Priest: The Holy Gospel of our Lord Jesus Christ, The lifegiving proclamation from St. (Matthew/John) the Apostle, who preaches the good news of life and salvation to the world.

OR

Priest: The Holy Gospel of our Lord Jesus Christ, The lifegiving proclamation from St. (Mark/Luke), the Evangelist who publishes the good news of life and Salvation to the world.

People: Blessed is he who has come and is to come: / Glory be to Him who sent Him for our salvation, / and may His mercy be upon us all, forever.

Priest: Now, in the time of the Dispensation of our Lord and our God and Savior Jesus Christ, the Word of Life, + God who took flesh of the Holy Virgin Mary, these things thus came to pass.

People: We believe and confess.

(The Priest reads the Gospel and concludes with the blessing)

Priest: Peace be unto you all.

INTERCESSORY PRAYERS - QUQLION

Pethgomo

(Makalilappan…)

As a father shows mercy to his children - Halleluiah
So the Lord shows mercy to those - who fear Him

As for man his days are like grass Halleluiah
Like the flower of the field – so he blooms. *Barekmor*

+ Glory be to the Father, Son and Holy Spirit
Unto the ages of ages and forevermore.

Eqbo

(Sharanaathale…)

May Your living voice awake
Your servants who slept in hope
And trusted in Your mercy
From the graves to paradise. *Stoumen kalos Kurielaison*

Qolo

(l'Maryam Yoldath Aloho/Rakshakane nin gaathrathe…)

O Savior, raise up the dead - who ate Your Flesh
And drank Your Blood, the Chalice of Salvation
Raise them up from the grave without corruption
And clothe them in glory, those who wait – for You…*Barekmor*

+ Glory be to the Father, Son and Holy Spirit

The Son of the King who gives life to the dead
Will be carried above the clouds of beauty
The righteous who hear the trumpet before Him
Will be clothed in glorious garments and meet Him
Lord have mercy upon us and help us.

Bo'utho of Mor Jacob

(Udhanathaal than sabhaye veendonaam puthra…)

Son who by Your resurrection redeemed Your Church
By it grant her and her children Your peace, O Lord

May Your peace stand guard at the corners of the Church
May Your love be a high fortress that protects her

O Lord, may Your peace guard her doors with diligence
May all those who come and cross its threshold find peace

Praise to the Father, who built His Church and guards it;
Worship to the Son whose death made a feast for her;

Thanks be to the Spirit who gathers and fills her
With praises from all people to the risen Son

Grant Your peace, which reconciled both heaven and earth,
To Your Church and keep her by Your Resurrection

(Trisagion Chanted to the Tone of the Day)

Holy art Thou, O God!
Holy art Thou, Almighty!
Holy art Thou, Immortal!
†Crucified for us, have mercy on us. *(Repeat Thrice)*

Lord, have mercy upon us,
Lord be kind and have mercy,
Lord, accept our service and our prayers
Have mercy on us.

Glory to You, O God!
Glory to You, Creator,
Glory to You, Christ the King
Who pities His sinful servants. *Barekmor*

Our Father, who art in heaven (p. 5)

COMPLINE of QYOMTHO [Sunday]

Qaumo (p. 5)

Introductory Prayer (p. 10)

QOLO

(Morahimin/Njan anchunen…)

I am afraid of my sins
That they may be - a wall, which keeps me
From the - Garden of delight,
Which is - kept for all the saints
Rescue me, O Lord, from hell
And where You will - there, Lord, let me dwell. *Barekmor*

+ Glory be to the Father, Son and Holy Spirit
Unto the ages of ages and forevermore.

Glory to You, Christ our King,
Who opens doors - to those who repent
I am - a sinner who begs
Of You, - Giver of good things
Gladden my heart by Your grace
That I may sing - as a harp to You
Lord have mercy upon us and help us

BO'UTHO of MOR BALAI

(Dushtanmaaril kaarunyam poondone…)

Lord, who has mercy even on sinners
Have mercy on us on Your Judgment Day!

At Your door O Lord, the afflicted knock
Answer their requests in Your compassion

Father in heaven, we do beseech You!
Accept our service; have mercy on us.

Lord of those above! Hope of those below!
Accept this service; have mercy on us

Kurielaison, Kurielaison, Kurielasion

Turn to ***Psalms of Compline (p. 10)***

NIGHT VIGIL of QYOMTHO [Sunday]

Qaumo (p. 5)
Introductory Prayer (p. 13)
Introductory Psalms of Night Vigil (p. 13)

ENIYONO

(Etheer Hathoyo/ Nammude rakshakanam

Together we rise – up from our slumber
And we sing praise
To our Savior who rose up – from the tomb on this morning

On this great Sunday – Our Lord Jesus Christ
Rose from the tomb
All the children of the Church – praise the Lord of creation

Upon this third day – O Messiah, who
Rose from the dead
Saved us from the pit of sin – and delivered us from death

Like prophet Jonah – the Lord spent three days
Within the earth
And on the third day the Lord – resurrected from the grave. *Barekmor*

+ Glory be to the Father, Son and the Holy Spirit
Unto to the ages of ages and forever more.

Let us sing praises – to the Son of God
Who rose from the tomb;
He who has no beginning – nor end triumphed over death

Kurielaison, Kurielaison, Kurielaison

Turn to the ***Introductory Prayer of 1st Qaumo (p. 14)***

1st QAUMO

EQBO

(Abo k'thab wo/Naadha sabhaye qymthayaal…)

Praise to the Lord who gladdened
The Church by His res*urrection*

Lord have mercy; Lord have mercy, Lord have mercy
(Kurieleison, Kurieleison, Kurieleison)

Lord, have mercy upon us
Lord, be kind and have mercy
Answer, Lord, and have mercy

Glory be to You, O Lord
Glory be to You, O Lord
Glory be to You, our hope forever. *Barekmor*

1st Qaumo - QOLO

(Abo k'thab wo/ Rakshakarane ninte mukham)

Lord, hide not Your face from us – enable us to rejoice
As the women did – when You rose from death
May we rejoice and enter – the bridal chamber with them…*Barekmor*

+ Glory be to the Father, Son and the Holy Spirit

May Your hands pierced with the nails – by the accurs`ed people
Raise us sinners up – from the sea of debts
May they raise us and make us – to ascend from the abyss

Unto to the ages of ages and forevermore.

Lord, may Your life-giving blood – shed for our absolution
Cleanse and purify – all our defilements
And may Your holy body – heal us and lead us to You

OR

1st Qaumo - QOLO

(Dahto lo Nehte/Vinulakin arachanmaar…)

The King of Heaven – founded His Church and
Made it His palace –and dwelt within it
Let all who wish to – speak to the Lord, come
For behold, He dwells – within the True Church
Halleluiah – Halleluiah
You Who sustain her – have mercy on us. *Barekmor*

+ Glory be to the Father, Son and the Holy Spirit
Unto to the ages of ages and forevermore.

The Holy Church which – is the Bride of Christ
Is like Paradise – full of all blessings
For within her is –Holy Baptism
And priests within her – bear holy myst'ries
Halleluiah – Halleluiah
And distribute the – medicine of life

Lord have mercy upon us and help us

BO'UTHO of MOR JACOB

Son, who raised and delivered Your Church from err`or
Grant her Your peace by Your bless`ed resurrection

The legions of light rose in honor of the King;
Gabr`i`el's company exulted before Him

The assembly on high came to see the Watcher
Who slept, awoke, and rose up at His own pleasure

Glory to the Hidden One who revealed Himself
Who suffered and died in the flesh and rose from death

The living and the departed shall confess you,
And Your Father above and Your Holy Spirit

Grant Your peace, which reconciled both heaven and earth,
To Your Church and keep her by Your resurrection

*Turn to the **Praise of the Cherubim** (p. 14)*

2nd QAUMO

*Turn to **Introductory Prayer of 2nd Qaumo** (p. 15)*

EQBO

(Sleq l'Sleebo/Vaagdanam pol jeevan…)

Bless`ed is Christ – who received life again
As He promised and gladdened creation

Lord have mercy; Lord have mercy, Lord have mercy
(Kurieleison, Kurieleison, Kurieleison)

Lord, have mercy upon us
Lord, be kind and have mercy
Answer, Lord, and have mercy

Glory be to You, O Lord
Glory be to You, O Lord
Glory be to You, our hope forever. *Barekmor*

QOLO

(l'Malkuth Rawmo/ Krushil thookichasehiyone nee…)

O Christ, we praise You – because You destroyed
That Jerusalem, – Which crucified Your body
You took the Church as Your bride
Therefore, she praises Your name
Along with all the nations
Because of – Your resurrection. *Barekmor*

+ Glory be to the Father, Son and the Holy Spirit
Unto to the ages of ages and forever more.

Guards saw the angels - who were clothed in white
Standing near the tomb - and ran to Jerusalem
To proclaim to the people
"Behold, the one you entombed
With seal and stone has appeared
And rose like - a flash of lightning
Lord have mercy upon us and help us

BO'UTHO of MOR EPHREM

Lord have mercy upon us
And compassion on the dead
Lord, by Your resurrection
You delivered us from sin

The accurs`ed ones sealed Him
That hero, within a grave -
Him who holds the ends of earth -
And who arose like lightning

The Lord broke open the tomb
And like a swimmer went forth
Whether He went up or down
His passage does not reveal

Lord, have mercy upon us
And compassion on the dead
Lord, by Your resurrection
You delivered us from sin

Turn to the ***Praise of the Cherubim (p. 15)***

3rd QAUMO

Turn to ***Introductory Prayer of 3rd Qaumo (p. 15)***

EQBO
(Abo k'thab wo/Karthave nalkashwaasam)

Give rest to our departed - in Your glor`i`ous abodes
Lord, give rest to them - and mercy to us
While You forgive and blot out - the faults of us and of them

Lord have mercy; Lord have mercy, Lord have mercy
(Kurieleison, Kurieleison, Kurieleison)

Lord, have mercy upon us
Lord, be kind and have mercy
Answer, Lord, and have mercy

Glory be to You, O Lord
Glory be to You, O Lord
Glory be to You, our hope forever. *Barekmor*

QOLO

(Bkhul Medem/Karthave ashwasam nalk'...)

Grant rest, O Lord, unto them
Our fathers and our brethren – have departed from this life
'Til resurrection comes for those who sleep
    Give rest, O Lord, to their souls in abodes of light
    May their bones quicken on the day of their mem'ry
        When Your command raises up
        All the children of Adam
May they be clothed with glory, - enter the bridal chamber
And offer praises to You, their Savior. *Barekmor*

+ Glory be to the Father, Son and the Holy Spirit
Unto to the ages of ages and forevermore.

Bless`ed are the dead for whom - the living make off`e`rings
For their mem'ries are written in heaven
    If Moses wrote the tribe's names on tablets of stone
    That they might have eternal mem'ry before God
        Lord, on the Host full of life
        Record the names of Your dead
That they may be remembered – in the Church and in heaven
And when the Lord comes they rejoice with him

Lord have mercy upon us and help us

BO'UTHO of MOR BALAI

Renew Your creatures by the res'rrection,
Your worshippers who have slept in Your hope.

    Give rest and pardon to the dead, O Lord,
    Who sleep in hope and await Your coming.

Lord, with Abraham, Isaac and Jacob,
Make Your servants rest, those who sleep in hope.

    Their bodies and souls shall cry together:
    "Bless'd is He who will come and raise the dead."

Turn to ***p. 16 to continue Night Vigil***

INTERCESSION OF THE MOTHER OF GOD - QUQLION

Pethgomo

(Ninnal sthuthiyodu raajamakal…)

The King's daughter stands in glory
Halleluiah (w halleluiah),
And the Queen at - Your right hand.

Leave your people and your father's house
Halleluiah (w halleluiah),
For the King will desi-re your beauty. *Barekmor*

+ Glory be to the Father, Son and the Holy Spirit
Unto to the ages of ages and forever more.

Eqbo

(Bhakthar pukazcha…)

O Pride of the faithful ones
Offer pray'rs on our behalf
To the Only Begotten
That He have mercy on us. *Stoumen kalos. Kurielaison*

Qolo

(l'Maryam Yoldath Aloho/Deivathin maatha...)

May mem'ry be made of the Mother of God
With the Prophets, Apostles, and the Martyrs
And the Children of the Church upon the earth
May Good mem'ry be made now and forever. *Barekmor.*

+ Glory be to the Father, Son and the Holy Spirit
Unto to the ages of ages and forever more.

Glory to the Son of God Who willed to come
From the womb of the Blessed Virgin Mary
And saved the people from error, by His Birth
Exalting her mem'ry; may her pray'rs help us.

INTERCESSION OF THE SAINTS - QUQLION

Pethgomo

(Nayavan panapole…)

The righteous shall flourish like a palm tree
Halleluiah (w halleluiah),
Like a cedar of Lebanon – he shall grow.

They shall flourish and be great in old age
Halleluiah (w halleluiah),
They shall be fruitful - and fragrant. *Barekmor.*

+ Glory be to the Father, Son and the Holy Spirit
Unto to the ages of ages and forever more.

Eqbo

(Orupolingum..)

Your mem'ry O St. (Thomas)
Be kept here and in Heaven
Let your pray'r be a help to
Those who honor your mem'ry. *Stoumen kalos, Kurielaison*

Qolo

(l'Maryam Yoldath Aloho/Prarthanayin samayamithallo...)

Behold, the time of pray`er, (O St. Thomas)
Stand and intercede at the head of your flock
Stretch forth your hand like Moses and bless all those
Who hasten to the sound of your gentle voice. *Barekmor*

+ Glory be to the Father, Son and the Holy Spirit
Unto to the ages of ages and forever more.

Praise to the Father Who chose you, St. (Thomas)
And to the Son Who honors your mem`o`ry
Worshipped is the Holy Spirit Who crowns you
By your pray'rs, may mercy be on us always

INTERCESSION OF THE FAITHFUL DEPARTED - QUQLION

Pethgomo

As a father shows mercy to his children
Halleluiah (w halleluiah),
So the Lord shows mercy to those - who fear Him

As for man, his days are like grass,
Halleluiah (w halleluiah),
Like the flower of the field - so he blooms. *Barekmor*

+ Glory be to the Father, Son and the Holy Spirit
Unto to the ages of ages and forever more.

Eqbo

May Your Living voice awake
From the graves to Paradise
Your servants who slept in hope
And trusted in Your mercy. *Stoumen kalos, Kurielaison.*

Qolo

(l'Maryam Yoldath Aloho/Rakshakane nin gathrathe...)

O Savior, raise up the dead who ate Your Flesh
And drank Your Blood, the Chalice of Salvation
Raise them up from the grave without corruption
And clothe them in glory, those who wait – for You. *Barekmor.*

+Glory be to the Father, Son and the Holy Spirit
Unto to the ages of ages and forever more.

The Son of the King who gives life to the dead
Will be carried above the clouds of beauty
The righteous who hear the trumpet before Him
Will be clothed in glorious garments and meet Him
Lord have mercy upon us and help us

Bo'utho of Mor Ephrem

(Karthave krupa cheyenamai)

Lord have mercy upon us
By Your mother's and saints' pray'rs

May the angel who brought peace
And announced to the virgin
Come and say to us that God
Is reconciled with us all

May the angel who sprinkled
Dew on the three holy youths
Sprinkle the dew of mercy
On the bones of all the dead

Lord have mercy upon us
By Your mother's and saints' pray'rs
Forgive all our offenses
And absolve our departed

Turn to the ***Hymn of the Angels (p. 20)***

MATINS of QYOMTHO [Sunday]

Qaumo (p. 5)

Introductory Prayer

† Glory be to the Father and to the Son and to the Holy Spirit.

May His grace and mercy be upon us, weak and sinful, in both worlds forever and ever. Amin.

Enlighten, Lord God, our eyes by the blessed rays of Your light and give us joy on the day of Your Resurrection from among the dead; make us glad by the manifestation of Your power and assist us by the help of Your grace, Christ, the hope of our lives and the Savior of our souls, our Lord and our God forever. Amin.

Turn to ***Psalm 51 (p. 21)***

ENIYONO

(Brikh dhadi l'shmayone/Mahimayoda kabareenapura…)

Bless`ed is the Light from Light: - Jesus, our Lord God
Who rose with glory and en-lightened creation

Simon Peter and John ran - to the tomb of Christ
And there they sang praises and - returned rejoicing

Today on this holy day, - the first-born of days
The First-born rose from death and - raised the earthly ones

Today the monasteries - and churches rejoice
For Christ rose and put to shame - His crucifiers

Today the spirits of the - departed rejoice
For Christ has sprinkled the dew - of mercy on them…*Barekmor*

+ Glory be to the Father, Son and Holy Spirit
Unto the ages of ages and forevermore.

Our Lord has said, "All who con-fess me shall not die"
We have confessed You. Raise us- to life by Your grace

Turn to ***Psalm 63 (p. 22)***

ENIYONO

(Qolo d'Shubho/Deivamuyarthu mahathwathodai…)

God rose from the dead in glory and raised to life
Adam and all his children
The angels praised their creator, the guards trembled,
And the earth was enlightened

Today, Simon Peter and John ran to the tomb
Of our Lord and our Savior
Today, Jacob rejoiced and Thomas exulted
Matthew was glad and sang praise

The Good Shepherd descended to She`ol and saved
His Church from idolatry
In glory He rose up like the Mighty One, and
Saved Her from her enemies

Today the Lord awoke from death like a warrior
Who has shaken off his wine (Ps. 78:65)
He killed death, demolished She`ol, and made it a
Footstool for all generations

Today God rose up from the dead and terrified
Those who stood guard at His tomb
They cried out in Jerusalem "Christ is risen!"
Which shamed His crucifiers. Barekmor

+ Glory be to the Father, Son and Holy Spirit
Unto the ages of ages and for ever more.

The righteous ones, who slept awaiting Your coming
Have today raised up their heads
They mourned until they saw Your light,which gladdened them
And they sang praise to Your grace

[Psalm 19] Kurielaison. The heavens declare the glory of God and the firmament proclaims His handiwork. / Day to day brings forth speech; / night to night declares knowledge;

There is no speech, nor are there words; their voice is not heard. / Yet their good tidings go out through all the earth,/ and their words to the end of the world.

In the heavens, He has set His tent for the sun, which comes out like a bridegroom leaving his chamber;/ it will rejoice like a strong man to run his course.

Its departure is from the end of the heavens / while its repose is at the end of the heavens and there is nothing hidden from its heat.

The law of the Lord is flawless and it turns the soul. / The testimony of the Lord is trustworthy and makes infants wise. / The commandments of the Lord are right and they make the heart rejoice. / The precepts of the Lord are chosen and they illumine the eyes.

The fear of the Lord is pure and it endures forever. / The judgments of the Lord are true and are more righteous than all. / They are more desirable than gold and even than precious stones. / They are sweeter than honey and the drippings of the honeycomb.

Moreover, Your servant will be warned by them; / If He keeps them, he will be greatly rewarded, but who can discern his errors? / Clear me from hidden faults.

Keep Your servant away from iniquity, lest the evil doers have dominion over me. / And I shall be purified from my sins. / O Lord, my helper and Savior, / let the words of my mouth be according to Your will / and the meditation of my heart be acceptable before You. / *And to You belongs praise, O God…Barekmor*

+ Glory be to the Father, Son and Holy Spirit
Unto the ages of ages and forevermore.

ENIYONO

(Shmayo m'ditho d'Malke/Mashiha jeevichezhunettu…)

Christ is ri-sen from the dead
Trampling down death by His death!
Rejoice O belov`ed Church!
And exalt the Living One

On Sunday, Simon Peter
And John ran to see the tomb
To confirm what they had heard
That their Master had risen

Reconcile with us, today,
The day of Resurrection
And forgive our offenses
By Your great loving kindness

Churches and monasteries
Offer praise this holy day
And sing glory and rejoice
In the Son's resurrection. *Barekmor*

+ Glory be to the Father, Son and Holy Spirit
Unto the ages of ages and for ever more.

God descended to She`ol
To raise the corrupt image
And renew fallen Adam
Who decayed and became old

[Isaiah 42:10-13, 45:8] **Kurielaison. Sing to the Lord a new song, His praise from the ends of the earth! Let those who go down to the sea in its fullness, the islands and their inhabitants, praise the Lord!**

Let the desert and its villages rejoice! Let Kedar be meadows; let the inhabitants of steep rocks praise Him! Let them shout from the top of mountains. Let them give glory to the Lord and declare His glory in the islands!

The Lord will go forth like a mighty man and like a warrior, He stirs up His fury; He will cry out and become mighty and will triumph over His enemies;

Let the clouds rain down righteousness; let the earth open and salvation increase; and let righteousness sprout forth altogether. I am the Lord who created them…*Barekmor*

+ Glory be to the Father, Son and Holy Spirit
Unto the ages of ages and forevermore.

ENIYONO

(Yaumono/Innal nin kabarinkal…)

Today the angels in white garb descended - to Your tomb
There they announced the glorious resurrection to the women, who
Brought spices and in-cense for You

Today we sing praise to You, who tasted death - by Your will
And who raised our race from the fall, joining us with those above so
That we might rejoice - with them all

On Sunday, angels stood at the tomb adorned - in white garb
One of them rolled the stone away and sat on it and announced to
The women that Christ - is risen. *Barekmor*

+ Glory be to the Father, Son and Holy Spirit
Unto the ages of ages and for ever more.

Today angels rejoice at Your resurrec-tion, O Lord
Simon sings praise and John exults for the women proclaimed the news
of Your glor'ious re-surrection

[Luke 1:46-55] **Kurielaison. Mary said, "My soul magnifies the Lord, and my spirit rejoices in God my Savior / because He has looked upon the lowliness of His handmaid; / for behold, from henceforth all generations shall call me blessed.**

Because He who is mighty has done great things for me and holy is His name. / And His mercy is from generation to generation on those who fear Him.

He has won victory with His arm, He has scattered the proud in the conceit of their heart. / He has put down the mighty from their thrones, and has exalted the lowly.

He has filled the hungry with good things and the rich He has sent away empty. / He has given help to Israel, His servant, mindful of His mercy / even as he spoke to our fathers, to Abraham and his seed forever...*Barekmor*

+ Glory be to the Father, Son and Holy Spirit
Unto the ages of ages and forevermore.

ENIYONO

(Lekh d'Kitho/Than mruthiyalazhakake...)

With voices befitting God,
We, the earthly ones, sing praise
To You who redeemed our race
From Satan's oppression and
Who by Your death put to death
The death that corrupts beauty. *Barekmor*

+ Glory be to the Father, Son and Holy Spirit
Unto the ages of ages and forevermore.

O Chosen and Holy Church
Gather your children for pray'r
Praise and glorify the Son
Who redeemed you by His Cross
With voices befitting God
We all sing praises to You

Turn to ***Psalm 113 (p. 23)***

ENIYONO

(Sogdeelokh/Maanavar vaanor mun mun nin…)

Angels and men worship You
Before Your great majesty.
Abundantly merciful,
Lord, to You befits glory

On the first day of the week
The doors of heaven opened
Hope and consolation came
For those sleeping in the dust

The creation rejoices
In Your Resurrection Lord
The departed in the tombs,
Whom You visited, praise You. *Barekmor*

+ Glory be to the Father, Son and Holy Spirit
Unto the ages of ages and for ever more.

On this holy day of the
Resurrection of the Christ
The Only Begotten rose
The earth and heaven rejoiced

ALTERNATE ENIYONO

(l'Haw Dat'ino/Yoodanmar kurishil thooki…)

The Jews- condemned, crucified and placed
Christ inside the tomb
They feared - that He might rise to life, which
would put them to shame
Halleluiah Halleluiah

They en-tombed the Mighty One who holds
The ends of the earth
But like -lightning He came forth without
Breaking the tomb's seal
Halleluiah Halleluiah

The Son - came to the vineyard seeking
Fruit from the workers
But they - seized and killed their Lord to take -
His inheritance
Halleluiah Halleluiah. *Barekmor*

+ Glory be to the Father, Son and Holy Spirit
Unto the ages of ages and forevermore.

Our Lord - came to creation seeking
All those who were lost
Yet they - seized and entombed Him, but He -
Rose and shamed them all
Halleluiah Halleluiah

[Matthew 5:3-12] **Kurielaison. Blessed are the poor in spirit, for the kingdom of heaven is theirs;**

Blessed are those who mourn, for they shall be comforted;

Blessed are the meek, for they shall inherit the earth;

Blessed are those who hunger and thirst for justice, for they shall be satisfied;

Blessed are the merciful, for they shall obtain mercy;

Blessed are the pure in heart, for they shall see God;

Blessed are the peacemakers, for they shall be called the children of God;

Blessed are those who suffer persecution for the sake of justice, for theirs is the kingdom of heaven;

Blessed are you when men reproach you and persecute you / and speaking falsely, say all manner of evil against you for my sake.

Rejoice and be glad because your reward is great in heaven…*Barekmor*

+ Glory be to the Father, Son and Holy Spirit
Unto the ages of ages and forevermore.

ENIYONO

(Ethdarkhrein bro d'Aloho/Naadha nin rajya…)

Lord, remember us - when You come in the
Great glory of - Your Kingdom, O Son of God

Make us worthy, Lord, - along with the thief
Of Your Kingdom - May we rejoice and sing praise

Raise us, Christ our King - to Your right-hand side
Along with the - thief who had believed in You

Lord, make us worthy - to inherit Your
Kingdom above - with the Saints who had pleased You

On this great day of - Your resurrection
O Christ our King – have mercy upon our souls. *Barekmor*

+ May we be worthy- to offer glory- honor, worship, and exaltation - to the Father, Son, and Holy Spirit.
Unto the ages- of ages and forevermore.

This Sunday, let us - worship and give thanks
To the Father, - Son, and the Holy Spirit…*Stoumen Kalos. Kurielaison.*

(Promion-Sedro is read)

QOLO

(Eno no Nuhro/Agnyathmeeyemaarrerum)

This day, the fi'ery angels
Descended to the Lord's tomb
Watchers of *fire* and spirit:
Cried aloud "Holy, Holy
God has risen from the grave
In glory and great pow`er"
And the guards trembled and fell
And they became like dead men
At the sight of the Watchers...*Barekmor*

+ Glory be to the Father, Son and Holy Spirit

The priests in*quired* of the guards
"Do the seals remain intact"?
With one voice all the guards said
"The seal remains unbroken
See for yourself the wonder,
which made us all like dead men
It may have been a vision
But we - cannot hide the truth,
which has been made known to us

Unto the ages of ages and forevermore.

Grant rest to our departed,
Those who have gone to their rest
Set Your worshippers among
The company of Your saints
    When You sit on Your throne to
    Divide the good from evil
    Let them behold Your mercy
May they - stand at Your right hand
When Your majesty appears
Lord have mercy upon us and help us.

(Etro is read)

QOLO

(Lokh Moriyo Qorenan/Daivathin puthranemariyam….)

In the garden, Mary saw the Son of God
She perceived Him Who had risen, as the gardener
He asked her "Why do you weep? Whom do you seek"?
"I weep for I do not know where they took my Lord"
    He called to - her say`ing 'Mary"
    Then she knew - the voice of her Lord
She ran to tell the apostles "Christ is Risen"! *Barekmor*

+ Glory be to the Father, Son and Holy Spirit

Praise to the Son of God, who rose from the grave
Who destroyed Zi`on and betrothed the Church instead,
He set within her a table of blessing
And for her mixed His living Flesh and precious Blood
    He redeemed - the Church by His Cross
    And gave life - to her by His death
Praise to Him who grants pardon through His Flesh and Blood

Unto the ages of ages and for ever more.

Let us beseech Christ for all the departed
Who ate His Body and drank His life-giving Blood
That the darkness of sin not reign over them,
Over their souls and their spirits in the Kingdom
    Lord receive - the spirits of those
    Who confessed - You and Your Passion
Call to them and raise them up at Your right hand side

INTERCESSION - QUQLION
Pethgomo

The King's daughter stands in glory —Halleluiah (w'Halleluiah)
And the Queen at - Your right hand.

The righteous shall flourish like a palm tree-
Halleluiah(w'Halleluiah)
Like a cedar of Lebanon - he shall grow.

As a father shows mercy to his children - Halleluiah (w'Halleluiah)
So the Lord shows mercy to those - who fear Him. *Barekmor*

+ Glory be to the Father, Son and Holy Spirit
Unto the ages of ages and for ever more.

Eqbo

Glory be to God on high
Honor be to His mother
Crowns of praise for His martyrs
Grace and mercy for the dead...*Stoumen Kalos, Kurielaison*

Qolo

(Shlomo d'Abo/Thaathan shlomo gabriel...)

The Father granted His peace
Unto the bless`ed virgin
Through the angel Gabr`i`el
He greeted Mary and spoke:
"The Lord is with you, Mary
And He shall come forth from you"...*Barekmor*

+ Glory be to the Father, Son and Holy Spirit

Peace be with all the prophets
Peace be with the apostles
Peace be with the bless'd martyrs
Who loved the Lord God of peace
Peace be with the Holy Church
In which the sons of peace dwell

Unto the ages of ages and forevermore

We remember our Fathers
Who taught us during their life
To be the children of God
The Son of God will grant them
Comfort along with the just
And the righteous in heaven
Lord have mercy upon us and help us.

BO'UTHO of MOR JACOB

(Udhanathaal than sabhaye veendonaam puthra…)

Son, who raised and delivered Your Church from er`ror
Grant her Your peace by Your bless`ed resurrection

When the hero slept on the Cross and trampled death
After three days, His sleep left and He rose strengthened

While He slept for three days His burden was lightened
From His labor He awoke without corruption

When He came forth, His forefather, David saw Him
And touched the strings of his harp to sing prophecy:

"He awoke like a war*rior* who shook off his wine
and struck His foes and delivered His friends who mourned"
(Ps. 78:65)

Grant Your peace which reconciled both heaven and earth
To Your Church and keep her by Your resurrection

(Trisagion Chanted to the Tone of the Day)

Holy art Thou, O God - Halleluiah
Holy art Thou, Almighty, - Kurielaison
Holy art Thou, Immortal,
†Save us Crucified One. *(Repeat Thrice)*

Lord, have mercy upon us, - Halleluiah
Lord be kind and have mercy, - Kurielaison
Lord, accept our service and our prayers
Have mercy on us.

Glory to You, O God! - Halleluiah
Glory to You, Creator, - Kurielaison
Glory to You, Christ the King
Who pities His sinful servants. *Barekmor*

Our Father, who art in heaven (p. 5)

THIRD HOUR of QYOMTHO [Sunday]

Qaumo (p. 5)

Introductory Prayer (p. 24)

QOLO

(Moriyo Moran/Udayone naadha nee udhanam cheythapol thottakaran....)

O Lord our Lord -
When You rose up from the grave– Mary saw You- as the gard`e`ner
She said to You:
"If you have taken the Son tell me where to - that I might take Him."
Then our Lord said:
"I am He who has risen, go tell this news - to My disciples" *Barekmor*

+Glory be to the Father, Son and Holy Spirit
Unto the ages of ages and forevermore.

On the first day
Which is the firstborn of days-Christ rose from death,-the firstborn of God
He raised with Him
Adam who is the firstborn – of all mankind- and made him ascend
Halleluiah
Praise to the Lord of Adam – who delivered – the sons of Adam
Lord have mercy upon us and help us.

BO'UTHO of MOR EPHREM

(Njangal than karthaave nee…)

Christ By Your Resurrection
You redeemed us and saved us
Lord, have mercy upon us
And upon our departed

On this Sunday, this great day
Hope and courage came to us;
The Living One rose from death
And shamed His crucifiers

On this Sunday, this great day
The Living One rose from death
He ascended and sat at
The right hand of His Father

Christ By Your Resurrection
You redeemed us and saved us
Lord, have mercy upon us
And upon our departed

Christ, who redeemed Your servants
By Your great Resurrection
Grant forgiveness to us, Lord
And to all our departed

Qaumo (p. 5)

SIXTH HOUR of QYOMTHO [Sunday]

Qaumo (p. 5)

Introductory Prayer (p. 25)

QOLO

(Thuro d'Seenai/Moschachamachora…)

Mount Sinai trembled – at Your presence Lord
Yet the Bless'd Virgin –
Carried You, Lord God who does
Carry the heights and the depths
Without marriage, she conceived
And wondrously, brought You forth
Magnify –her mem'ry, O Lord. *Barekmor*

+ Glory be to the Father, Son and Holy Spirit

Saints are invited – To the High Kingdom
And eternal life – that which ear has never heard
Nor has the eye of flesh seen
Nor the heart of men conceived
Bless'd are those worthy of it
The Noble - ones who have loved Christ

Unto the ages of ages and for ever more.

Those who are sealed in - holy baptism
with the seal of Christ
Who ate His holy Body
And drank His atoning Blood
Shall be raised up from the dust
To life eternal and shall
be clothed in - garments of glory

Lord have mercy upon us and help us.

BO'UTHO of MOR BALAI

(Maatha kadeeshenmar than prarthanayal...)

Lord, by the pray'r of Your mother and saints,
Have mercy on us and our departed.

May Mary's mem'ry be for our blessing,
And may her pray'r be a refuge for us.

Prophets, Apostles, and holy Martyrs,
Beseech and beg for mercy for us all.

Sprinkle the dew of gladness on the heads
Of our departed who sleep in Your hope.

Praise to Him who has honored His mother,
Glorified the saints, and raised up the dead.

Lord, by the pray'r of Your mother and saints,
Have mercy on us and our departed.

Qaumo (p. 5)

NINTH HOUR of QYOMTHO [Sunday]

Qaumo (p. 5)

Introductory Prayer (p. 27)

QOLO

(Lo l'Deeno w'Lo Lathba'atho – Deivathin jeevaathmajane kaikelilenthi)

With the bless`ed martyrs and confessors who loved You
And with all the saints
O Lord, make mem'ry of our departed ones
Make them stand at Your right hand
Halleluiah, and grant rest to them…*Barekmor*

+ Glory be to the Father, Son and Holy Spirit
Unto the ages of ages and forevermore.

Our Savior heard the groan of the departed upon
The height of the cross
He hastened to come and break the yoke of death
From the necks of those who slept
Halleluiah, and comforted them

Lord have mercy upon us and help us!

BO'UTHO of MOR BALAI

Renew Your creatures by the res'rrection,
Your worshippers who have slept in Your hope.

Give rest and pardon to the dead, O Lord,
Who sleep in hope and await Your coming.

Lord, with Abraham, Isaac and Jacob,
Make Your servants rest, those who sleep in hope.

Their bodies and souls shall cry together:
"Bless'd is He who will come and raise the dead."

Qaumo (p. 5)

VESPERS of DAY TWO [Monday]

Qaumo (p. 5)... Introductory Prayer (p. 8)... Psalms of Vespers (p. 8)

EQBO

(Htith Bashmayo - Swargathodum ninnodum)

I have sinned in Your sight and am not worthy
To be called Your son.
Accept me into Your house as a servant
Because I - have sinned. *Staumen Kalos Kurielaison*

QOLO

(Qabeloy Moran - Snehasametham vishwasathode)

In love and in faith
Our Lord, please accept
This incense from us like the incense - of Aaron,
Which kept death from the people...*Barekmor*

+ Glory be to the Father, Son and Holy Spirit
Unto the ages of ages and forevermore.

Glory to You, Lord
Whose praise is above in heaven and - on the earth.
Those in both worlds praise Your name.

On the Theotokos

The Archangel brought
A greeting of peace to the daughter – of David:
'The Lord shall come forth from you.'

The bush, which Moses
The prophet, saw on Sinai was an – image of
Mary, the The`o`tokos

On the Saints

Prophets, Apostles,
You sons of the Kingdom, pray that we – are not drowned
In the troubled sea of sin.

Martyrs saw the Son,
Who stretched His hands on the Cross and due – to His love
They surrendered to torture

On Repentance

The Lord is faithful in His words
We call upon You
Answer us as You promised. Accept – our service.
In Your mercy hear our pleas.

Pray without ceasing.
And let us not grow weary while there - is still time
To seek mercy from our Lord

On the Departed

Christ, full of mercy,
Let Your sweet voice be heard by those who – lie in dust
Who were clothed in baptism

Give rest, O Savior
To Your faithful servants who have slept – in Your hope
On the day of Your coming.
Lord have mercy upon us and help us!

QOLO

(Lo Ldino/Moran yeshu mashiha-Nadha ninthanuvum ninavum…)

Our Lord Jesus Christ
Let not - Your Body and Blood we have received
Be for judgment nor condemnation
But for pardon and resurrection
And grant us unveiled faces
Halleluiah – before You, Lord… *Barekmor*

+ Glory be to the Father, Son and Holy Spirit
Unto the ages of ages and forevermore.

O Lord – may Your Body, which we have consumed
And Your living Blood we drank in faith
Be a bridge and passage, which saves us
From the *fire* and Ge`henna
Halleluiah – and grants us life

On the Theotokos

Behold, - the virgin who was able to bear
Him who bears both the heavens and earth
Intercedes with Him for us sinners
May her pray'r be with us all
Halleluiah – who call on her

Let there – be mem'ry made of the bless'd virgin
The Mother of God who bore for us
In her virginity, Christ the King
The Savior of creation
Halleluiah – we seek your pray'rs

On the Saints

Simon – the head of the Holy Apostles,
Paul the Chosen, and John the Baptist,
Pray for the flock, which You fed with the
Waters of faith and lead it
Halleluiah – to the pasture

Martyrs - were el`o`quent clusters who stood firm
Before the judges and they were pressed
Like grapes and their blood flowed on the earth
As a sacrifice to God
Halleluiah - who honored them

On One Saint

Father – O St. (Thomas), you are like a tree
That sprouts up by a stream of water,
Whose head reaches up to heaven and
Whose fruits give help to mankind!
Halleluiah – Pray for our sake!

On Sunday

Taste and see how good the Lord is
On this – Sunday, which has passed You gave to me
Your Body and Blood to eat and on
That Sunday, which does not pass away
Make us worthy to praise You
Halleluiah - at Your right hand

On Repentance

David – prophesied and said, "The Lord will come
And He will heal the broken-hearted,"
So Christ used waters of baptism
To heal our hearts broken by
Halleluiah – our sinfulness

O Lord – have mercy on us! Lord, have mercy!
Lord, receive our service and our pray'rs
May Your grace, which stood by the martyrs
And strengthened them in their *trials*
Halleluiah – rest upon us

On the Departed

Give rest – and remembrance to the departed
Who ate Your Body, O Son of God
Grant them unveiled faces to meet You
When Your Coming is revealed
Halleluiah – that they praise You

Our Lord – heard the groaning of the departed
On top of the tree on Golgotha
And was moved to break the yoke of death
From the necks of those who slept
Halleluiah – and gave them rest

PETHGOMO

(Tone 6 - Lenkanamukthi labhichavanum)

Bless`ed is he whose in`i`quity is forgiven – Halleluiah
And whose sins are hidden

Because I was silent, my bones wasted away – Halleluiah
While I cried out all the day. *Barekmor*

+ Glory be to the Father, Son and Holy Spirit
Unto the ages of ages and forevermore.

EQBO

(Bhawbay Wahtohay - En kadapaapangal...)

I confess my sins – and my offences
And I beg of You – have mercy on me
Stoumen Kalos Kurielaison

QOLO

(Lo Ldino - Manuja snehi nee sandhya)

In the – evening Abraham - called upon You
On the – mountaintop and You
Answered, - O lover of men. - In the evening
We call - upon You, O God
Halleluiah - for Your mercy…*Barekmor*

+ Glory be to the Father, Son and Holy Spirit
Unto the ages of ages and forevermore.

While the - soul and body are - in this world they
Call You - for Your compassion
When they - are separated - they cannot beg
For the - pardon of their sins
Halleluiah - forgive them both

Lord have mercy upon us and help us!

BO'UTHO of MOR JACOB

O Lord, our Lord, - we call to You - come to our aid
Hear our requests - and have mercy - upon our souls

In the evening - when the sun's light - sets upon earth
May I be en-lightened to praise - Your creation
Son of God, may - Your word be a - lamp to my feet
And in place of - the sun may I - walk by its light

In the evening, offer thanks and - pure pray'r in love
Instead of all sacrifices - and burnt-off'rings
The one who possesses a mouth - and word and tongue
Ought to give thanks for the creatures, - which are silent

The evening has placed me in the - watch of the night.
Lord, be the sun by which I walk - in the evening

Turn to ***Concluding Prayer of Vespers (p. 9)***

COMPLINE of DAY TWO [Monday]

Qaumo (p. 5)... Introductory Prayer (p. 10)

QOLO

(Lthumo d'haimonootho – Ekathmaja deva njaa nin)

My sins are many, O God
And my faults have gained strength so I gaze upon
Your sea of mercy
I cry out to You, O Lord
Sprinkle me with Your hyssop and wash me in
The tears of my eyes
By the love of Your Father
Do not let my en`e`mies mock me, rather
Lead me to confess
That the angels may rejoice
Over one sinner who repents of his faults
And let them proclaim
Bless`ed is He who opens
His door to those who repent - Halleluiah
By night and by day...*Barekmor*

+ Glory be to the Father, Son and Holy Spirit
Unto the ages of ages and forevermore.

Lord, look upon my weakness
For I have sinned greatly and have angered You
And find no refuge
I approached the physicians
Who tried medicines on me but the abscess
Remains infected
Good Physician, I have heard
That he who approaches You receives Your help
With Your medicine
By the love of Your Father
And the pray'rs of Your mother – Halleluiah
Forgive all my sins

Lord have mercy upon us and help us!

BO'UTHO of MOR EPHREM

Lord, have mercy upon us
O Lord receive our service
Send us from Your treasure-house
Mercy, grace, and forgiveness

Let not your body stand there
While your heart is distracted
May your body be a church
Your mind, a sanct`u`ary

May your mouth be a censer,
Your lips like smoke of incense,
And your tongue a minister,
Which pleases the Trinity

Lord, who hears our petitions
Answer us in Your mercy
Lord, be reconciled with us
Have compassion upon us

Kurielaison, Kurielaison, Kurielaison

Turn to ***Psalms of Compline (p. 10)***

NIGHT VIGIL of DAY TWO [Monday]

Qaumo (p.5)…Introductory Prayer(p.13)…Introductory Psalms(p.13)

ENIYONO

(A'ir mor d'amkoothan – Udayonam naadha)

Wake and raise me up
From the forgetful slumber to the – praises of
Your majesty, O Lord God

I know the watchers
Never slumber and like them I have – risen up
I praise You, Lover of Men

I know I have sinned
In my sorrow my tears have flowed; par-don my sins
Lord, let Your mercy be moved

By night, I recalled
Your most holy name and I rise to – give You thanks
And praise You, Lover of men

My sins are many
And they confront me at the dread seat – of judgment
Lord, let Your mercy be moved

In Zi`on above
And in the Church here on earth, Lord make – mem`o`ry
Of those who rest in Your hope…*Barekmor*

† ***Glory to the Father, Son, and Holy Spirit.***
Unto the ages of ages and forevermore.

Glory to You, Lord
Whom the watchers cannot look on but – the earthly
Adam holds You in his hands

Kurieleison, Kurieleison, Kurieleison

Turn to ***Introductory Prayer of 1st Qaumo (p. 14)***

1st QAUMO

EQBO

(Abo k'thab wo)

My bones shall cry from the grave – a virgin has brought forth God
If I doubt may I – be cast out from truth
If there is doubt in my mind – into hell may I be cast

Lord have mercy; Lord have mercy, Lord have mercy
(Kurieleison, Kurieleison, Kurieleison)

Lord, have mercy upon us
Lord, be kind and have mercy
Answer, Lord, and have mercy

Glory be to You, O Lord
Glory be to You, O Lord
Glory be to You, our hope forever. *Barekmor*

QOLO

(Quqoyo)

O virgin, your mem'ry is a benediction
Respond to the pleas of those who are far and near;
  Those who are sick – grant healing to them
  Those in distress – grant comfort to them
Drive away the devil from those whom he torments
By your pray'rs and pleas may mercy be shown to us
  Halleluiah – May your prayer help us…*Barekmor*

† Glory to the Father, Son, and Holy Spirit.
Unto the ages of ages and forevermore.

I know not how to call you, daughter of David;
Nor do I know what name to give you, O Mary
  You are 'virgin' – yet you nurse the Son
  You are 'mother' – yet remain virgin
Therefore, I will call you the mother of our God
That the learn`ed and the doubters be put to shame
  Halleluiah – Woe to the doubters

Lord have mercy upon us and help us

BO'UTHO OF MOR JACOB

O bless`ed one, may your pray'rs be with us always
May the Lord hear your pray'rs and have mercy on us

  The bless'd virgin called me that I should speak of her
  Let us cleanse our ears that her story be honored
  Second heaven, in your bosom the Lord rested
  And came forth to drive away darkness from the earth

Daughter of the poor, you were the mother of God
And gave wealth to the world in need that it might live
Ship, you carried the treasures of the father's house
And came and poured out your wealth on our barren earth

By the pray'r of her who carried you for nine months
O Son of God, remove from us the scourge of wrath

Turn to ***Praise of the Cherubim (p. 14)***

2nd QAUMO

Turn to ***Introductory Prayer of 2nd Qaumo (p. 15)***

EQBO

(Abo k'thab wo)

You are the saintly heroes – who conquered the kings of earth,
Not by swift arrows – nor by sharpened swords,
But by the pow'r of the cross – slew the *error* of the demons

Lord have mercy; Lord have mercy, Lord have mercy
(Kurieleison, Kurieleison, Kurieleison)

Lord, have mercy upon us
Lord, be kind and have mercy
Answer, Lord, and have mercy

Glory be to You, O Lord
Glory be to You, O Lord
Glory be to You, our hope forever. *Barekmor*

QOLO

(Quqoyo)

Moses is the symbol of the old covenant;
Peter the new, and both resemble the other
Moses brought down – tablets with the law
Peter received – keys to the kingdom
Moses constructed the earthly tabernacle
And for the new, Simon Peter built up the Church
Halleluiah – May their pray'rs help us…*Barekmor*

† Glory to the Father, Son, and Holy Spirit.
Unto the ages of ages and forevermore.

John, the preacher of truth, Stephen and Theodore;
George the Martyr and warr'iors Sergius and Bacchus;
Kur`i`akose – and St. Julitta;
Shamouni and – her seven children;
The forty holy martyrs of Seb`ast`ia
And St. (Thomas) – all holy, elect ones of God
Halleluiah – May your pray'rs help us

Lord have mercy upon us and help us!

BO'UTHO OF MOR EPHREM

Lord have mercy upon us
By the pray'rs of Your servants
By their pray'rs and petitions
Have mercy upon our souls

Make mem'ry, Lord and Savior
Of the prophets, apostles
The martyrs, and the righteous
And help us by their pray`ers

Glory be to the Strong One
To Him who strengthened you all,
Prophets, apostles, *and* Martyrs
Who won vict'ry by the cross

Lord have mercy upon us
By the pray'rs of Your servants
By their pray'rs and petitions
Have mercy upon our souls

*Turn to **Praise of the Cherubim (p. 15)***

3rd QAUMO

*Turn to **Introductory Prayer of 3rd Qaumo (p. 15)***

EQBO

(Abo k'thab wo)

Standing at the outer door – Peter bitterly shed tears:
"Lord, open Your door – to Your disciple
Heav'n and earth will weep for me – I lost the keys of heaven"

Lord have mercy; Lord have mercy, Lord have mercy
(Kurieleison, Kurieleison, Kurieleison)

Lord, have mercy upon us
Lord, be kind and have mercy
Answer, Lord, and have mercy

Glory be to You, O Lord
Glory be to You, O Lord
Glory be to You, our hope forever. *Barekmor*

QOLO

(Quqoyo)

Your servants shall give thanks to You Lord, Halleluiah
In the night let us rise and thank the Son of God
For by night there will be a cry that the Lord comes
  Just and righteous - prophets, apostles,
  And bless'd martyrs - will go to meet Him
Ent'ring with Him the marriage chamber full of joy
They will inherit life and the kingdom and sing
  Halleluiah - to the glorious Lord...*Barekmor*

† ***Glory to the Father, Son, and Holy Spirit.***
Unto the ages of ages and forevermore.

In the midst of night David arose to give praise
For the wonders of the most High and His judgments
  He saw heaven - and the firmament
  He saw the stars - and their fair courses
He saw the peace and the calm of the creation
His soul filled with awe and he gave thanks to You, Lord
  Halleluiah - for its great marvels

Lord have mercy upon us and help us

BO'UTHO of MOR BALAI

Lord, who has mercy even on sinners
Have mercy on us on Your judgment Day!

  At Your door O Lord, afflicted ones knock
  Answer their requests in Your compassion

Father in heaven, we do beseech You!
Accept our service - have mercy on us.

  Lord of those above! Hope of those below!
  Accept this service - have mer-cy on us

Turn to ***p. 16 to continue Night Vigil***

Qolo of the Day

(Quqoyo)

God has called me to the festival of St. (John)
If I go, I'll fear; If not I will be afraid
If I go, I – will recall my sins
If I do not – I will be estranged
By the blood which flowed forth from the Son of God's side
Pardon my offenses and may your pray'rs help us
Halleluiah – Glory to the Lord…*Barekmor*

+ Glory be to the Father, Son and the Holy Spirit
Unto to the ages of ages and forever more.

The Church calls you bless`ed, O St. (Gregorios)
The blessing of our Lord was imparted to you
Bless`ed are you – who hated this world
Bless`ed are you – who longed for Christ's love
Bless`ed are you, when you shall hear the voice of Him:
'Come, inherit the kingdom and eternal life'
Halleluiah – May your prayer help us

Lord have mercy upon us and help us

BO'UTHO OF MOR JACOB

O Lord, our Lord, we call to You come to our aid
Hear our requests and have mercy upon our souls

In the dark of night David awoke to sing praise
To give thanks for the great wonders of the godhead
Now, you also rise in the middle of the night
With the psalms of David chant praises of spirit

By Your rad`i`ance, Lord, May I be enlightened
For you are as the day for the ones who love You
The way of the world is a net full of all snares
He who walks by You is safe for You are the day

Answer O Lord, Answer O Lord, and have mercy
Turn the hearts of the sons of men to repentance

*Turn to **Hymn of the Angels (p. 20)***

MATINS of DAY TWO [Monday]

Qaumo (p. 5)... Introductory Prayer (p.21)... Psalms of Matins (p.21)

ENIYONO

(Lawothokh Qadmen – Vannen vandhichen...)

I stand before You
I worship before Your throne, O Lord, - of heaven
Forgive my sins a-gainst You

I rose this morning
To confess my faults to You, O Lo-ver of men
Forgive my sins a-gainst You

As You drew Simon
From the raging of the sea, O Lord – draw Your Church
From all schisms and disputes

O Light, Son of Light,
Who dwells in the light; Make me worthy – of that light
Which darkness cannot con-sume

O Lord, I received
Your Flesh and Blood, which pardoned all my – offences
Do not leave me in She`ol

At the morning hour
The light gladdens creation and all – those in it
Offer praise and thanks-giv-ing

I beg of You, Lord
I long for Your mercy, O good and – gentle one
Pardon my sins a-gainst You ...*Barekmor*

+ Glory be to the Father, Son and Holy Spirit
Unto the ages of ages and forevermore.

Glory to You, Lord
Whose praise is above in heaven and – on the earth.
Those in both worlds praise Your name...*Amin*

Turn to ***Psalm 113 (p. 23)***

EQBO

(l'Qolo d'Shubho-Naadha dhoothasthuthi naadhathaal nin sthuthi paadaan)

Lord, awaken me to the hymns of the angels
That I may sing Your praises
In the morning, I open my mouth to praise You
My Lord and God have mercy. *Stoumen Kalos Kurieleison*

QOLO

(Anin Moriyo/Karthave prarthana kettarul – Halleluiah)

Answer me, Lord, and hear my pray'r, Hal-leluiah
Receive our incense like that, which Aaron offered
As You did in Nineveh, receive our service
And as You answered Jonah
Answer us who call on You...*Barekmor*

+ Glory be to the Father, Son and Holy Spirit
Unto the ages of ages and forevermore.

Glory to the mercy of Your grace, Lord Jesus
For Your great bounty flows out over the whole world
When the Ninevites called You
You delivered them from wrath

On the Theotokos

From the ranks of *fire* a Watcher flew to Mary
And announced to her say`ing "The Lord is with you"
And He shall come forth from you,
The Savior of Creation"

As *fire* rested on the bush, the bush was not burnt
So God descended and rested in the virgin
He chose to take flesh from her
Guarding her virginity

On the Saints

The martyrs hated the goods of this passing world
They renounced their fathers, brethren, and their nation
They chose death for Jesus' sake
Their mem'ry is glorified

The martyrs saw Christ, their Lord, hanging on the wood
From His side pierced by the lance, blood and water flowed;
They encouraged each other:
"Come let us die for our Lord"

On Repentance

By Your light we see the light Jesus, full of light
You are the True Light, which enlightens all creatures,
Shine Your joyous light on us
O Splendor of the Father

Come all sinners beg and plead for your forgiveness
If you knock at the Lord's door it will be opened
If you ask you shall receive
If you seek then you shall find

On the Departed

Pardon all the sins of our fathers and brethren
Who have slumbered and reposed, O Lord, in Your hope
Write all of their names in the
Book of Life in Your Kingdom

Lord, make good mem'ry of the faithful departed
Who consumed Your Holy Body and Living Blood
Make them stand at Your right hand
On that day Your glory dawns

Lord have mercy upon us and help us.

QOLO

(Bsafro Nqadem – Abraham bali nalkiyapol)

Rich and poor- together
By morning let us hasten
To pray'r like our father Abraham
That we may see Christ on that great morning
May He come and say to us:
"Come in peace good and faithful servants
Inherit the kingdom and lasting life." ...*Barekmor*

+ Glory be to the Father, Son and Holy Spirit
Unto the ages of ages and forevermore.

The night passed as is written
And the day has approached and has come
Awake my brethren and rise up to pray
Our Lord said in His Gospel:
"To him who calls Me, I will answer
To him who knocks, I will open the door

On the Theotokos

Christ came forth from the Father
And from the bless'd Daughter of David.
From Bethlehem came the True Bread of Life
Worshipful is the Father
Who sent His only-begotten Son
Bless'd is Mary who gave birth to our Lord

As I passed by Bethlehem
Behold I heard a voice in a cave
It was Mary singing hymns to her Son
She sang: "Bless'd am I, my Son
Who became Your mother and nursed You
Your grace has allowed me to approach You".

On the Saints

Our Lord sent twelve physicians
To the four corners of creation
And told them to drive out demons from men
The Lord also ordered them
To go out and heal those who are sick
"Freely you received, freely give of it."

Glory to the Son of God
Who has pow`er on both sea and land
And chose simple men to be His preachers
From the sea He chose Peter
And from the road He called Paul to Him
He made them builders of the Holy Church

On One Saint

O Bless`ed St. (Anthony)
Beg for mercy for the assembly
Which celebrates your mem'ry on your feast
May the Lord bestow His peace
And His tranquility upon us
With fruitful years from His rich treasure-house

On Repentance

"I did not come for the just
Said our Lord, "But I came for sinners,
That they may turn their hearts to repentance".
Behold the door of the Lord
Is open. Sinners repent and live
For God said, "I do not desire your death."

Bless`ed is he who forgives
When his brother has offended him
For God will also show mercy to him
Our Lord said in His gospel
"Bless'd are the merciful, for mercy
Shall be on them at the resurrection."

On the Departed

Isaac prepared Abraham
To be buried while he wept and mourned
For no one knew of the resurrection
God revealed it to Moses
And He showed to him these hidden things:
How the righteous live forever in God

I sought wealth I cannot take
I sought for the beauty, which decays
I sought friends and they profited nothing
I enter the judgment place
Where brother cannot save his brother
Save me Lord, for this thought terrifies me

PETHGOMO

(Tone 2 – En vachanangale naadha sradhichen… - Halleluiah)

Hear my words, O Lord, and consider my meditation – Halleluiah
Hear the voice of my cry, my King and my God

For it is to You I pray – Halleluiah
Lord, in the morning You shall hear my voice…*Barekmor*

+ Glory be to the Father, Son and Holy Spirit
Unto the ages of ages and forevermore.

EQBO

(Bnayo D'abo – Swarga pithaavin aathmajare)

Sons of the Father in heav'n,
You who do the will of God,
Praise and exalt the Lord and bless Him
Now and forever. *Stoumen Kalos, Kurieleison*

[Monday – Sapro]

QOLO

(Men Abo – Kahalanaadhathodu kaala)

In the morning, trumpets blew
The walls of Jericho fell, while the Israe'lite people
Cried the Lord is God
In the morning raise your voice
My brethren sing praise to God that He may have mercy on
The enti`re world…*Barekmor*

+ Glory be to the Father, Son and Holy Spirit
Unto the ages of ages and forevermore.

In heaven and on the earth
Angels and the sons of men worship Your majesty while
They cry out and say:
"Ho-ly are You, O God
Holy are You, Almighty! Holy are You Immortal!
Who did redeem us

Lord have mercy upon us and help us!

BO'UTHO of MOR JACOB

Open unto us, Your great door full of – mercy
Lord, hear our pray'r and have mercy upon our souls

Shine on me, Lord, and I shall be light like – the day
I will sing Your praise in the light while I marvel
May morning awaken me to praise Your – Godhead
And I will study Your word all throughout the day

With the day may – Your light shine up-on all our thoughts
And drive a-way – the shadows of – sin from our souls
Creation is – full of light, give – us light also
That our hearts may– praise You with the- day and the night

Light which gives life to all creatures in the – morning
Give light to our minds that we may thank you, O Lord!

Turn to ***Concluding Prayer of Matins (p. 23)***

THIRD HOUR of DAY TWO [Monday]

Qaumo (p. 5)... Introductory Prayer (p. 24)

QOLO

(Quqoyo – Swarga pithave nin makkalku...)

When I sin I hide myself so that no one sees
Yet I cannot hide from God who sees all my deeds
Why am I shamed – if a man sees me
But have no fear – of my Lord and God?
Whether I die soon or live longer in this life
I will be delivered to the Judge of judges
Halleluiah – have mercy on me...*Barekmor*

+ Glory be to the Father, Son and the Holy Spirit
Unto the ages of ages and forevermore.

I grieve knowing that I am Yours only in name
For my deeds and faults reveal I am far from You
Though I long to – confess and repent
My stubborn pride – does not allow me
I teach but do not learn; I give drink yet I thirst
Quench my thirst, O Spring, which was opened by the lance
Halleluiah – that I may be filled

Lord have mercy upon us and help us!

BO'UTHO of MOR JACOB

O Lord, our Lord, we call to You, come to our aid
Hear our requests and have mercy upon our souls

I beg that I not be separated from You
Sin drove me out; but let Your sweet love welcome me
Sin lay in wait and it crushed me without mercy
Physician, bind up the bruises, which wounded me

Glory to You, Good Shepherd who redeemed Your flock
And descended to rescue the sheep that was lost;
Who, among men, is able to praise Your glory,
You who abide in the Father with the Spirit?

Answer, O Lord! Answer O Lord, and have mercy
Turn the hearts of the sons of men to repentance

Qaumo (p. 5)

SIXTH HOUR of DAY TWO [Monday]

Qaumo (p. 5)

Introductory Prayer (p.25)

QOLO

(Lo l'Deeno wLo Lathba'atho, Deivathin jeevathamajane kaikelilenthi)

Mary stands among the assemblies and carries the –
Living Son of God
She gives milk to the Providence who feeds all –
The creatures by a gesture
Halleluiah, May her pray'r – help us…*Barekmor*

+ Glory be to the Father, Son and the Holy Spirit

Behold, how heaven and earth rejoice at your mem'ry -
O bless`ed martyrs
Angels and men are gladdened and sing praise to -
The pow'r, which rests in your bones
Halleluiah, May your pray'rs – help us

Unto the ages of ages and forevermore.

May the dew, which descended on the furnace in the
Land of Babylon
And delivered the young men from the fi`re,
Deliver our departed
Halleluiah – May they re-ceive life

Lord have mercy upon us and help us!

Turn to ***Bo'utho of Mor Balai (p. 25)***

NINTH HOUR of DAY TWO [Monday]

Qaumo (p. 5)... Introductory Prayer (p. 27)

QOLO

(Hwilo l'Nafesho, Snanam thanil ninne...)

You, who have slept in corruption, rise up from the dust;
The Great King, your resurrection, will come in glory
And shake off the
Dust from your faces and will clothe you – in glor'ious garments.
Barekmor

+ Glory be to the Father, Son and the Holy Spirit
Unto the ages of ages and forevermore.

The voice, which cried out to Adam: "Return to the dust,"
Has passed, and another says: "Come forth like Lazarus
And leave the grave".
For now is the time when those exiled – return to Eden
Lord have mercy upon us and help us!

BO'UTHO of MOR BALAI

Renew Your creatures by the res'rrection,
Your worshippers who have slept in Your hope.

Give rest and pardon to the dead, O Lord,
Who sleep in hope and await Your coming.

Lord, with Abraham, Isaac and Jacob,
Make Your servants rest, those who sleep in hope.

Their bodies and souls shall cry together:
"Bless'd is He who will come and raise the dead

Qaumo (p. 5)

VESPERS of DAY THREE [Tuesday]

Qaumo (p. 5)... Introductory Prayer (p. 8)... Psalms of Vespers (p. 8)

EQBO

(Sli Moriyo Brahme/Naadha kriypayal cheivichayi…)

Incline Your ear in mercy
And hear the voice of my pray'r
Be pleased to kindly receive
Our service and our pray`ers. *Staumen Kalos Kurielaison*

QOLO

(Qabeloy Mor/Swargathilumingoozhiyilum – kaikollaname)

In heaven and on the earth
Glory to You
Son who sits at the right hand while all – the angels
Cry, 'holy, holy' to You…*Barekmor*

+ Glory be to the Father, Son and the Holy Spirit
Unto the ages of ages and forevermore.

I have entered
Your house and worshipped before Your throne – O Great King
Pardon my sins against You

On the Theotokos

Virgin Mary
Your story is beyond what our words – can express
For you bore the Lord of all

By the pray'rs of
The virgin who bore You, take away – from Your Church
The scourge and the rod of wrath

On the Saints

At all times we
Remember prophets, apostles, and – bless'd martyrs
May their pray'rs be our refuge

Martyrs who passed
By the bridge of *fire* to the heights, pray – we not drown
In the raging sea of sin

On Repentance

"Repent, repent!"
Said our Lord that when the groom comes you – may enter
The bridal chamber with Him

O God, my heart
Is ready, O God, my heart is re-ady to sing
Praise to You by night and day

On the Departed

May those who sleep,
And confessed the Trinity stand at – Your right hand
Lord, at Your second coming

O Christ, who raised
Laz`a`rus of Beth`a`ny, raise the – departed
Purchased by Your precious blood
Lord have mercy upon us and help us!

QOLO

(Hwilo l'Nafesho/En rakshaadhipanaam naadha...kenivazhiyanisham…)
O Lord God my salvation
Be the protector of my soul, O Lord – because I
Walk among the snares of worldly pleasures – every day
Save my soul, Lord – Deliver me from my faults
By Your grace – For You love – mankind...*Barekmor*

+ Glory be to the Father, Son and the Holy Spirit
Unto the ages of ages and forevermore.

Be my shield and I shall be delivered – from the fire
Do not let the flames consume me and burn – all my limbs
Have mercy, Lord – Sprinkle me with the dew, which
Protected – the youths in – the *fire*

On the Theotokos

Gabr`i`el descended on the wings of – the Spirit
He came to Mary and brought greetings and – said to her
"Peace be with you – for the Lord, the Savior, is
With you and – shall come forth – from you"

Mother of God, we take refuge in you – every day
We take shelter in your pray'r, which is a – great fortress
Pray to your Son – that His tranquility and
His peace dwell – throughout the – whole world

On the Saints

Bless`ed is Christ, who built the Holy Church – on His hands
And placed as her foundation the prophets, - apostles,
And the martyrs. – He filled her with all peoples
Who offer – praise by night – and day

O, You bless`ed martyrs who were slain for – our Savior
And whose blood rose like incense before the – throne of Christ
Pray to your Lord – that His tranquility and
His peace dwell – throughout the – whole world

On One Saint

O Holy St. (Ephrem), you are a good – example,
Of watching, and fasting, and praying by – night and day
May the faithful – imitate your example
As they seek – enrichment – from God

On the Church

Earth! O Earth! Hear the Lord's promise He made- to His Church:
"I vow that I will never leave you nor – forsake you
O Faithful Church– At all times I guard your walls
And I will – always dwell – in you"

On Repentance

I knock at the door of Your mercy, Lord – forgive me
The cunning ways of the evil one have – kept me from
The path of life – and have kept my mouth from praise
And my feet – from the Ho-ly Church

"O how this world has deceived me!" cried out – the rich man.
"Its pleasures have passed like a dream, now hell – torments me
I am denied - water in this sea of *fire*.
Woe to me – I do not – repent!"

On the Departed

Death gloated over the dust of our fa-ther Adam
And over his fair beauty consumed by – corruption
Our Lord saw him – and was grieved and descended
To restore – Adam by – the Cross

The voice from the top of the tree, which shook – creation
Shall call and wake up from the dust those who – sleep in Christ
They shall be clothed – in a garment of glory
On that day – of the Lord's – coming

PETHGOMO

(Tone 6 – Vaazthuka naadane en aathmave)

Bless the Lord, O my soul – Halleluiah
And all my bones bless His holy name

Bless the Lord, O my soul – Halleluiah
And forget not all His benefits…*Barekmor*

+ Glory be to the Father, Son and the Holy Spirit
Unto the ages of ages and forevermore.

EQBO

(Go'en Bishe/Erithikuzhiyil Dushthenmar)

The wicked cry from the midst of the *fire* like the rich man
They ask for a drop of water but none gives what they ask
    Your com-passion is greater
    Than our – in`i`quity, Lord
Forbid that eternal *fire*
From consuming Your – image. *Stoumen Kalos Kurielaison*

QOLO

(Hwilo l'Nafesho/Shaanthi prathamaam…)

Bless'd is He who has given us an e-vening of peace
And a night of repose when the weary – workers rest
    And glo-rify the Father,
    The Son, - who redeemed our race
    And the – Holy Ghost…*Barekmor*

+ Glory be to the Father, Son and the Holy Spirit
Unto the ages of ages and forevermore.

Bless`ed is the man who keeps his faults be-fore his eyes
Like David, the righteous king and the glo-r'ious prophet
    Who cried – in his repentance
    "O God – have mercy on me
    And for-give my fault"

Lord have mercy upon us and help us!

BO'UTHO of MOR JACOB

O Lord, our Lord, - we call to You – come to our aid
Hear our requests – and have mercy – upon our souls

When the Son of – God comes at the – second coming
It will not be – by the Cross as – it was in the
First coming when – He came as a – sacrifice but
He will come to – pass judgment – when He comes again.

He will try the world like gold in a – crucible
And the fi`re will burn any im-purity
Be fearful my brethren, when the Son – of God comes
Let us hasten to take refuge in – repentance

Christ before whom my imperfections - are revealed
In the *hour* when You judge me O Lord – have mercy

*Turn to **Concluding Prayer of Vespers (p. 9)***

COMPLINE of DAY THREE [Tuesday]

Qaumo (p. 5)

Introductory Prayers (p.10)

QOLO

(Qtilo D'aqtal/Aadatheyaho)

O You the slain – who by Your slaying slew both
Death and Satan
Slay the sin, which – dwells in me and makes me its
Slave by my will
O Good Shepherd – who went in search of
Sheep that strayed from – the flock and was lost
O seek for me – who am lost like the one coin
Out of ten, which –
The woman lost – and did seek
Because You are – He who finds those who are lost
Halleluiah praise – be to You...*Barekmor*

+ Glory be to the Father, Son and the Holy Spirit
Unto the ages of ages and forevermore.

Fear not sinner – to turn back and walk the way
Of repentance
For Your Lord has – gone out in search of you and
If He finds you
He will rejoice – and forgive your sins
Like He forgave – the sinful woman
He will stretch His – hand to you as to Peter
And grant to you-
As to the thief – Paradise
He will rejoice – and bear you on His shoulders
Halleluiah and – embrace you

Lord have mercy upon us and help us!

BO'UTHO of MOR JACOB

O Lord, our Lord, - we call to you - come to our aid
Hear our requests - and have mercy - upon our souls

The sinner is - loved when his face - is bathed in tears
And his mouth is - closed by mourning - full of sorrow
The tears, which flow - from the eyes of - him who repents
Are cherished and- loved much more than-all precious gems

If you wish to - paint a picture - of repentance
You must add - your sorrowful tears - to the colors
Tears are a feast - of repentance, - come and bring them
Come and enjoy - forgiveness for - your debts and sins

Answer O Lord - Answer O Lord - and have mercy
Turn the hearts of - the sons of men - to repentance

Kurielaison, Kurielaison, Kurielaison

Turn to ***Psalms of Compline (p. 10)***

NIGHT VIGIL of DAY THREE [Tuesday]

Qaumo (p.5)... Introductory Prayer (p.13)... Psalms of Night (p.13)

ENIYONO

(Eth'eer l'hathoyo/ Paapi unaruka nee)

Awake, O sinner – while there is still time
For repentance
Cleanse and purify your stains – with mournful tears and sighing

If you wish your debts – to be forgiven
Cry unto God
With passion call upon Him – and He will forgive your fault

O mighty Lord, who – redeemed all mankind
From its bondage:
The slavery of our sin – Lord of all, glory to You

May Your right hand, Lord – which parted the sea
Before the host
Open the door of mercy – to our petitions and pray'rs

Let our departed – abide in the light
With all the saints:
In tabernacles of light – where there is no death or pain…*Barekmor*

+ Glory be to the Father, Son and the Holy Spirit
Unto the ages of ages and forevermore.

We offer to You – a pure thanksgiving
And a new praise
And to You we cry aloud – Lord of all, to You be praise

Kurieleison, Kurieleison, Kurieleison

*Turn to the **Introductory Prayer of 1st Qaumo (p. 14)***

1st QAUMO

EQBO

(Honaw Yarho)

The bless'd virgin – has called me to – tell her story
And I am now full of wonder
Son of God, grant me Your wonder
That I may fa-shion an image – of Your mother

Lord have mercy; Lord have mercy, Lord have mercy
(Kurieleison, Kurieleison, Kurieleison)

Lord, have mercy upon us
Lord, be kind and have mercy
Answer, Lord, and have mercy

Glory be to You, O Lord
Glory be to You, O Lord
Glory be to You, our hope forever. *Barekmor*

QOLO

(Lok Moriyo Qorenan)

The Queen is at your right hand, halleluiah
Behold, your name, Mary is honored on earth
Who would not honor you since Christ magnified you
Palace of holiness in which the king dwelt
O, new heaven which was carry'ing God the Word
  In your arms - you embraced the flames
  You gave milk - to the burning fire
Bless`ed is the infinite who was born of you...*Barekmor*

+ Glory be to the Father, Son and the Holy Spirit
Unto the ages of ages and forevermore.

Bless`ed are you, the pride of all creation
Pure virgin and holy mother of the Most High
For the Word of the Father took flesh from you
He was born of you yet kept your virginity
  Bless'd are you - you destroyed the curse
  Of- Eve - mankind's first mother
We gained salvation through you; may your pray'r help us
Lord have mercy upon us and help us!

BO'UTHO of MOR JACOB

O bless`ed one, may your pray'rs be with us always
May the Lord hear your pray'rs and have mercy on us

  Who is this virgin who stands above the whole world
  And will not suffer darkness to rule over it?
  It is Mary, who in her person is like day
  And when she speaks, the sun rises forth from her lips

May that veil, which shed light on the pathway of earth
Make intercession and offer pray'rs before God
She proclaims to her Lord and her Son and her God
"Have mercy on the world for which you endured death"

By the pray'r of her who carried you for nine months
O Son of God, remove from us the scourge of wrath

*Turn to **Praise of the Cherubim (p. 14)***

2nd QAUMO

*Turn to **Introductory Prayer of 2nd Qaumo (p. 15)***

EQBO
(Honaw Yarho)

Praise the Strong One– who bless'd martyrs– and strengthened them
Bless'd be He who has honored them
And magnified them throughout earth
Bless`ed is He - who poured His love - into their hearts

Lord have mercy; Lord have mercy, Lord have mercy
(Kurieleison, Kurieleison, Kurieleison)

Lord, have mercy upon us
Lord, be kind and have mercy
Answer, Lord, and have mercy

Glory be to You, O Lord
Glory be to You, O Lord
Glory be to You, our hope forever. *Barekmor*

QOLO
(Lok Moriyo Qorenan)

Lord, why do you not hear Your suff'ring servants?
David was persecuted and Isaiah sawn;
Daniel was thrown in the den and John was slain;
Zachariah was sacrificed at the altar;
Shamouni - and all her children
Were sent to - the court of justice
You who give justice to the oppressed, have mercy…*Barekmor*

+ Glory be to the Father, Son and the Holy Spirit
Unto the ages of ages and forevermore.

When the martyrs entered the court of justice
They were clothed in the spiritual armor of Christ
They were strengthened by faith, stood fast with courage
And were not shaken by tortures or by torments
    On the earth - they were victor'ious
    In heaven - they were triumphant
Jesus, full of mercy, keep us under their wings

Lord have mercy upon us and help us!

BO'UTHO of MOR EPHREM

Lord have mercy upon us
By the pray'rs of Your servants
By their pray'rs and petitions
Have mercy upon our souls

    Make mem'ry, Lord and Savior
    Of the prophets, apostles
    The martyrs, and the righteous
    And help us by their pray`ers

Pray for us, O holy ones
To the One whose will you did
That He may withdraw from us
The scourge and the rod of wrath

    Lord have mercy upon us
    By the pray'rs of Your servants
    By their pray'rs and petitions
    Have mercy upon our souls

*Turn to **Praise of the Cherubim (p. 15)***

3rd QAUMO

*Turn to **Introductory Prayer of 3rd Qaumo (p. 15)***

EQBO
(Honaw Yarho)

Woe be to me - for I have been - among the just
        But I have profited nothing
        Because I have not learned their ways
I am estranged - and now my sin - keeps me from them

Lord have mercy; Lord have mercy, Lord have mercy
(Kurieleison, Kurieleison, Kurieleison)

Lord, have mercy upon us
Lord, be kind and have mercy
Answer, Lord, and have mercy

Glory be to You, O Lord
Glory be to You, O Lord
Glory be to You, our hope forever. *Barekmor*

QOLO

(Lok Moriyo Qorenan)

Hear, Lord, the voice of my petition, Halleluiah
At night I thought of You, Lover of mankind
And upon my bed I meditated on You
I see my stains and I fear to call on You
But I gain strength by the thief and the publican
Along with – the sinful woman
They tell me – to be encouraged,
'To approach because our Lord is full of mercy'…*Barekmor*

+ Glory be to the Father, Son and the Holy Spirit
Unto the ages of ages and forevermore.

By night awaken my heart, O Son of God
That I may sing praise and thanksgiving for Your grace
The evil one wishes to drown me in sin
He drowns me in sleep that I may not sing Your praise
Strengthen me – that I might rise up
And praise You – for Your compassion
And I will cry aloud glory to You, O Lord
Lord have mercy upon us and help us!

BO'UTHO of MOR BALAI

Renew Your creatures by the res'rrection,
Your worshippers who have slept in Your hope.

Give rest and pardon to the dead, O Lord,
Who sleep in hope and await Your coming.

Lord, with Abraham, Isaac and Jacob,
Make Your servants rest, those who sleep in hope.

Their bodies and souls shall cry together:
"Bless'd is He who will come and raise the dead."

*Turn to **p. 16 to continue Night Vigil***

QOLO of the SAINT of the DAY
(Lok Moriyo Qorenan)

Like a merchant, who chooses good pearls to sell
The noble St. (Ephrem) chose fasting and pray`er
For vigilance and pray'r are pleasing to God
And behold, His Lord, when He saw his way of life
He bestowed – upon St. (Ephrem)
The power – to heal his brethren
That he might heal the diseases of Adam's race…*Barekmor*

+ Glory be to the Father, Son and the Holy Spirit
Unto the ages of ages and forevermore.

Two great lights entered the Church of believers
The bride of Christ, St. Ephrem, the noble elder
And that sea of wisdom, Jacob of Sarug
Together they filled the whole earth with their wisdom
Their teaching – confirmed the true faith:
The myst'ry – of the Trinity,
In the Father, the Son, and the Holy Spirit
Lord have mercy upon us and help us!

BO'UTHO of MOR EPHREM

Lord have mercy upon us
O Lord, receive our service
Send us from Your treasure-house
Mercy, grace, and forgiveness

Like those virgins, may we watch
For Your coming in the night
That with them we may enter
The heav'nly bridal-chamber

Let us not be drowned in sleep
Let us keep watch at the door
That with Him we may enter
The heav'nly bridal-chamber

You who hear and answer prayers
Show Your kindness to us all
Hear our pray'rs and our requests
And answer us, O Lord God

*Turn to **Hymn of the Angels (p. 20)***

MATINS of DAY THREE (Tuesday)

Qaumo (p. 5)…Introductory Prayer (p.21)…Psalms of Matins (p.21)

ENIYONO

(Nuhro d'Olmo – Jagadeepthi deivathanujaa)

O light of the world – O Son of our God
I rose before You, have mercy

O Jesus, our God – O You, the True Light
I rose before You, have mercy

I know I have sinned – and therefore, I cry
I rose before You, have mercy

Due to all my sins – and my many faults
I rose before You, have mercy

O Lord, Who is pleased – with those who repent
I rose before You, have mercy

O Christ, the image – of Your great Father
I rose before You, have mercy

O Resurrection – and hope of the dead
I rose before You, have mercy…*Barekmor*

+ Glory be to the Father, Son and the Holy Spirit
Unto the ages of ages and forevermore.

The One who is wor-shipped – in three Persons
I rose before You, have mercy. Amin.

Turn to ***Psalm 113 (p. 23)***

EQBO

(Bhaw Nuhro Gayo – Shuba thejasil maalaakhamar)

All the angels serve – Your God-head
In – the – joyous light
And at morning all – creation
Hastens to worship – You, Lord. *Stoumen Kalos, Kurieleison*

QOLO

(D'dahto lo Nehte – Praatha kaalathil dhoopam vekumbol)

Lord in the morning you shall hear my voice, halleluiah
In the morning when – incense is offered
The angels on high sing praises to You
The priests in splendor – offer sweet incense
For the sake of our sins and offenses
Halleluiah w'Halleluiah
Lord, answer them and respond to their pleas…*Barekmor*

+ Glory be to the Father, Son and the Holy Spirit
Unto the ages of ages and forevermore.

Glory be to Christ – who sat by the well
Seeking water from the Sama`ri`tan
She would not give it – and He caused to flow
The medicine of life, which quenched her thirst
Halleluiah w'Halleluiah
And the blood from His side redeemed the Church

On the Theotokos

O bless`ed mother – intercede for us
With your only Son who came forth from you
That in His mercy – He blot out our sins
And at His coming He does not judge us
Halleluiah w'Halleluiah
May your pray'rs be our stronghold and refuge

The bush, which Moses – saw on Mount Sinai
Represented you O holy virgin
The bush signified – your holy body
And the unburnt leaves, your virginity
Halleluiah w'Halleluiah
The *fire* was God who dwelt in your body

On the Saints

Glory to Christ who – built upon His hands
The Church and set up the altar in it
And set the prophets – apostles and the
Martyrs who triumphed as its foundation
Halleluiah w'Halleluiah
Bless'd is He who built and confirmed His Church

Tell me, O Martyrs – what did you expect
That you let your flesh endure such torments?
"We hoped for that, which – the eye has not seen
Nor what ear has heard nor entered the heart
Halleluiah w'Halleluiah
That which God promised to those who love Him

On One Saint

The afflicted who– take refuge in you
Chosen St. (Peter) answer their requests
Heal those who are sick – and cleanse the lepers
And set free those tempted by the demons
Halleluiah w'Halleluiah
May your pray'r be our refuge and stronghold

On the Morning

If this morning, which – is passing away
Drives away darkness and lightens the world
How great will it be – on that morning when
Our Lord comes again and raises the dead
Halleluiah w'Halleluiah
You who crown Your worshippers, have mercy!

On Repentance

Let him who has sinned – go and sin no more
And let him who has not sinned be watchful
Justice holds a pen – and stands at the door
And writes everyone's deeds impartially
Halleluiah w'Halleluiah
You who know all hidden things, have mercy!

By my will I sin – and by it, repent
I know the reason Satan has caught me
Woe to me for I – have sinned against You
Woe to me for I am not repentant
Halleluiah w'Halleluiah
Woe to me when you judge; Lord have mercy!

On the Departed

Make mem'ry of the - faithful departed
Let us not forget those who have left us
Let us write their names - at the Lord's altar
That at all times the Lord will give them rest
Halleluiah w'Halleluiah
May they worship You, their Resurrection

Since Adam transgressed - his Lord's commandment
Death fell upon all those born of woman
Praise to Him who gave - this cup to the world
That all drink from it and pass from this world
Halleluiah w'Halleluiah
Bless'd is he who rejects this world's pleasures

Lord have mercy upon us and help us!

QOLO

(Shlomo d'Abo - Deivathin thiruvishtam pol - praarthanakalkayi)

According to the will of God
On the morning of our Lord
His salvation shall appear-
He will reward the righteous
Bless'd is he who has labored
In the vineyard of his Lord-
For he will be rewarded... *Barekmor*

+ Glory be to the Father, Son and the Holy Spirit
Unto the ages of ages and forevermore.

At the time of the morning
Those above and below praise-
Him, who sits at the right hand,
By whose command the darkness
Death and Satan were destroyed-
Your light reigns over the world

On the Theotokos

The peace of God, the Father
Was sent down to bless'd Mary-
By the hand of Gabr`i`el
The *fiery* one announced peace
And said, "The Lord is with you-
And he shall come forth from you."

Mary was filled with wonder
At the words which *Gabriel* spoke-
She understood that the Lord
Would dwell in her and she said:
"I am the hand-maid of God-
Let it be as the Lord wills."

On the Saints

Peace be with you, O Prophets
Peace be with you, Apostles-
And peace be with you, Martyrs
You, who loved the Lord of Peace
Peace be with the Holy Church-
In which the sons of peace dwell

Martyrs, you did not enter
The arena by yourselves-
For your Lord entered with you
And gave courage to your minds
And when He saw your true love-
He magnified your mem'ry

On One Saint

Our father, St. (Severus)
You gained feathers and swift wings-
Feathers will lead to vict'ry
By the wings you will ascend
You will go to meet your Lord-
By your life of perfection

On Repentance

O Lord, may Your kingdom come
May Your will be done on earth-
As it is done in heaven
Forgive us our offences
Keep all temptation from us-
Deliver us from evil

O thief, speak of the beauty
Of paradise for our sakes-
And show us the tree of life
That we may pluck its first-fruits
Of watching, fasting, and pray'r-
And righteous sacrifices

On the Departed

In a place full of gladness
And the marriage-feast of joy -
Give rest, O Lord, by Your grace
To the faithful departed.
Refresh them in that kingdom -
Which shall never pass away

Upon Your servants O, Lord
Who were baptized in Your name,-
And obtained for their journey
Your Body and Holy Blood,
Have compassion when You come-
And clothe them in glor'ious garb

PETHGOMO

(Tone 8 – Neechanmaar ila suya)

Do not be env'ious of the evildoers - Halleluiah
And do not be jealous of those - who do wrong

For like the grass they shall quickly wither - Halleluiah
And like the herbs of the grass - they shall fade...*Barekmor*

+ Glory be to the Father, Son and the Holy Spirit
Unto the ages of ages and forevermore.

EQBO

(B'edon Safro – Praathkaalath aadyum srishtikalandathaye)

At the time-of-morn-ing - creation worships
Him who drives darkness from it and she sings praise:
"Glory to You, O God". *Stoumen Kalos, Kurieleison*

QOLO

(Praavinu vittu pulariyilapralayathil)

At the time of the morning
Righteous Noah sent a dove
Which returned to the ark for
The waters had subsided
It carried an olive branch
The sign of peace and goodwill...*Barekmor*

+ Glory be to the Father, Son and the Holy Spirit
Unto the ages of ages and forevermore.

At the time of the morning
A bow of *fire* was seen in
The sky as a sign of peace
And the mouth of God promised
"I will not flood earth again
From henceforth and forever"
Lord have mercy upon us and help us!

BO'UTHO of MOR EPHREM

(Maanjidumi praathakalath)

On this morning, which passes
Lord, have mercy upon us
On that morn, which does not pass
Make us stand at Your right hand

At morning, the creatures come
And knock at Your door, O Lord
To seek from Your treasure-house
Mercy, grace, and forgiveness

From each morning to morning
I have sought Your salvation
On that morning when You come
Make us stand at Your right hand

As the dove came to Noah
Bearing a branch of olive
So may our pray`er return
With compassion and mercy

Turn to ***Concluding Prayer of Matins (p. 23)***

THIRD HOUR of DAY THREE [Tuesday]

Qaumo (p. 5)…Introductory Prayer (p. 24)

QOLO

(Mshiho Natareh)

Our Lord spoke in parables and taught in allegories:
"The kingdom of heaven is like those virgins who went forth
And the virgins took their lamps
To meet the bride – and the True Bridegroom
And a great cry was uttered, "Behold the Bridegroom has come!
The wise entered with their Lord into the banquet
But the foolish ones remained at the door with deep sighs – and in great sorrow…*Barekmor*
+ Glory be to the Father, Son and the Holy Spirit
Unto the ages of ages and forevermore.

The kingdom on high is like a man who made a great feast;
And he called for the people but they would not come to it
So he sent out his servants
To summon all – to rejoice with him
From all places they gathered and the house was filled with guests;
He went out to them and found a man among them
Who was not dressed for the feast and was told to be cast- into the darkness
Lord have mercy upon us and help us

BO'UTHO of MOR JACOB

O Lord, our Lord, we call to You, come to our aid
Hear our requests and have mercy upon our souls

The sick soul says in her pain: "Who will clothe me with
That beauty, which I was clothed in before I sinned?
If God who is merciful will not accept me,
Who shall restore to me that beauty, which I lost?

My soul, image of the king, you lost your beauty
But in your Lord's hands your beauty is kept for you
The moment you return He will give it to you
He has kept it for you that it may be restored

Answer O Lord, answer O Lord, and have mercy
Turn the hearts of the sons of men to repentance

Qaumo (p. 5)

SIXTH HOUR of DAY THREE [Tuesday]

Qaumo (p. 5)... Introductory Prayer (p. 25)

QOLO

(Shlomo d'Abo)

Gabr'iel came down like lightning
To Mary and spoke softly:
"Peace be unto you, Mary,
For the Lord is upon you;
Pow'r from on high will join you,
The Spirit shall dwell in you" ..*Barekmor*

+ Glory be to the Father, Son and the Holy Spirit

O Apostles and Martyrs
Be our stronghold and refuge
Against all evil forces;
May those who honor your bones,
Be bless'd by your entreaties,
And inherit the Kingdom.

Unto the ages of ages and forevermore.

May the dead be remembered,
May the living have good hope;
Let us give glory and praise,
To the Father of mercies,
For He is our Lord and God,
Hope of the living and dead.

Lord have mercy upon us and help us!

Turn to ***Bo'utho of Mor Balai*** *(p. 25)*

NINTH HOUR of DAY THREE [Tuesday]

Qaumo (p. 5)... Introductory Prayer (p. 27)

QOLO

(Lok Moriyo Qorenan)

O You who have died in Christ, do not be grieved,
Behold the reward and resurrection has come;
From your graves, you shall rise without corruption,
And go forth in haste to meet the Son of the King;
Putting on - garments of glory,
You shall sing - praises before Him;
You, who raise up the sons of Adam, have mercy...*Barekmor*

+ Glory be to the Father, Son and the Holy Spirit
Unto the ages of ages and forevermore.

My brothers, it is true that death is bitter;
The *hour* of departure is painful and dreadful;
Thought ceases when dread angels surround the soul,
And the eyes are overcome with tears of sorrow;
The body - does not mourn the soul,
The soul mourns - over the body;
Lord, have mercy on both at the resurrection

Lord have mercy upon us and help us!

BO'UTHO of MOR BALAI

Renew Your creatures by the res'rrection,
Your worshippers who have slept in Your hope.

Give rest and pardon to the dead, O Lord,
Who sleep in hope and await Your coming.

Lord, with Abraham, Isaac and Jacob,
Make Your servants rest, those who sleep in hope.

Their bodies and souls shall cry together:
"Bless'd is He who will come and raise the dead

Qaumo (p. 5)

VESPERS of DAY FOUR [Wednesday]

Qaumo (p. 5)... Introductory Prayer (p. 8)... Psalms of Vespers (p. 8)

EQBO

(Lekh nethkashaf / Yacheekunnu...)

We beseech you,
O The`o`tokos, that you may intercede
To Christ our God,
The true King of kings, that He may grant His peace
To dwell in all the world
And remove rods of wrath
In His great mercy. *Staumen Kalos Kurielaison*

QOLO

(Am etro d'besme/Nathane vazthun...)

Praise the Lord, you righteous ones!
With this sweet incense - let mem'ry be made
Of Virgin Mary - the The`o`tokos. *Barekmor.*

+ Glory be to the Father, Son and Holy Spirit
Unto the ages of ages and for ever more.

With this sweet incense - let mem'ry be made
Of teachers and priests - the just and righteous

Theotokos

May Mary's mem'ry - be for our blessing
May her pray'r be a - fortress for our souls

Behold, sweet fragrance - rises in the air
For Virgin Mary - the The`o`tokos

Saints

Bless'd are the Prophets - and the Apostles
Bless'd are the Martyrs - at Resurrection

Martyrs who desired - to behold the Christ
By the sword, gained wings - and flew to the heights

Repentance

Do not judge us, Lord - who judges justly
Do not remember - all our offences

Come, Lord, to our help - strengthen our weakness
Our hope is in You - by night and by day

Departed

In Zi`on above – at the throne of Christ
May mem'ry be made – of the departed
Lord have mercy upon us and help us.

QOLO

(Lokh Moriyo Qorenan/Vaanilu …)

In Heaven, Earth and Eden – Halleluiah
May a good mem'ry be made of the Virgin
In churches and monasteries through-out the world
She was pure and holy in virginity
Pleasing to the King of Kings who dwelt – in her womb
Her mem'ry- is in heav'n and earth
May her pray'r – be for our refuge
Lord, make us share in the mem'ry of – Your mother. *Barekmor*

+ Glory be to the Father, Son and Holy Spirit
Unto the ages of ages and for ever more.

Glory to the Son of God, who was so pleased
To come forth from the bless`ed and ho-ly virgin
Through her ear she received Him and she bore Him
He came forth from her womb and yet it - remained sealed
Praise to Him – Who humbled Himself
Praise to Him – Who did become Man
Praise to Him who saved His Church and she – sings His praise!

Saints

Pray for us Apostles to Him Who chose you
That schisms and disputes cease in the – Holy Church
See! Heretics surround her on ev'ry side
To conceal the faith which you proclaimed – unto her
May Your truth – be a crucible
Which refines – her words like pure gold
May priests in victr'y praise Him who ma-gnified her

O Martyrs, you saw Him who hung on the Cross
Sitting at the right hand of God wea-ving your crowns
Therefore you thought nothing of ev'ry torture
And cleansed your limbs in the blood, which flowed–from your necks
Bless'd are you – who trampled all pain
And did yearn – for the love of Christ
Your mem'ries are honored in heaven – and on earth

A Saint

O St. (Luke) wise physician to whom our Lord
Gave the authority to heal the – afflicted
We take refuge in the fragrance of your bones
By your pray'rs may all our petitions – be answered
    Grant complete – healing to the sick;
    And refresh- those who are weary;
Grant return to those afar and par-don our sins

Repentance

Come to our help, O Lord, we call upon you
For the evil one troubles the world – by his craft
He has stirred up war among judges and kings
He tries to deceive even those who – are righteous
    What shall we – take our refuge in
    If not in – Your loving-kindness
Drive away the evil one by Your – Holy Cross

Judge of judges at the seat of Your judgment
Do not make me bow my head for my – offences
By which I have sinned and I have angered You
And if I am not worthy of Your – forgiveness
    Have mercy – because within me
    Is buried – Your Body and Blood
I have loved You and a-dored Your Cross, Lord Jesus

Departed

O You who have died in Christ, do not be grieved,
Behold the reward and resurre-ction has come
From your graves you shall rise without corruption
And go forth in haste to meet the Son – of the King
    Putting on – garments of glory
    You shall sing - praises before Him
You, Who raise up the sons of Adam, - have mercy!

PETHGOMO

(Tone 7 – Ninnal sthuthiyodu raajamakal)

The king's daughter stands in glory– Halleluiah w`Halleluiah
And the queen at - your right hand

Leave your people and your father's house –Halleluiah w`Halleluiah
For the king will desire - your beauty...*Barekmor*

+ Glory be to the Father, Son and Holy Spirit
Unto the ages of ages and forevermore.

EQBO

(Dethfni – Aardrathayal daasi)

He looked with mercy on - His handmaid's affliction,
He Who exalts His mother - and is the One Holy God
Stoumen Kalos Kurielaison

QOLO

(Lok Moriyo Qorenan – Chonnal mariyam ninshakthya ninne vahichen)

Mary said, "You strengthened me to carry You.
When I bore You in the cave, I saw - Your glory
The Seraphim fly above Your little crib
Command them to raise their wings that I, - may enter
To kneel down - and worship You, Lord
At Your crib - surrounded by flames
I will give to You pure milk, which shall please Your will."...*Barekmor*

+ Glory be to the Father, Son and Holy Spirit
Unto the ages of ages and forevermore.

In the law and the prophecies of Moses
Are found the types which prefigured the - bless'd mother:
The ark of the law, and the pot of manna;
Aaron's staff, which budded in the ta-bernacle;
The dew and - fleece of Gid`e`on
The wondrous - jar of Elisha
And the cloud of light of glor`i`ous - Isaiah

Lord have mercy upon us and help us!

BOU'THO of MOR JACOB

Make us share, Lord in Your mother's - and saints' mem'ry
By their pray'rs have mercy on us- and on our dead

We beseech you Mary the Daugh-ter of David
You have freedom to approach the - King of all kings
We beseech you, Virgin Mary, - pearl without flaw
To intercede with that fruit, which - came forth from you

Take courage, O Departed, who - dwell in the tombs
There is Good News: the resurrec-tion has drawn near
The Word, which formed you in the womb - will call on you
And will raise up your bodies with-out corruption

May mem'ry be made in heaven - and in the Church
Of the Virgin, saints, and the faith-ful departed

*Turn to **Concluding Prayer of Vespers (p. 9)***

COMPLINE of DAY FOUR [Wednesday]

Qaumo (p. 5)

Introductory Prayers (p.10)

QOLO

(Bkhul Medem/Akhilam njan aranjittu…)

All things I have con-sidered – Nothing have I seen better
Bless'd is he who loved - the fear of the Lord
Joseph the just loved it and became king of - Egypt
Moses loved it and divided the sea with – his staff
Daniel and his friends loved it
And it saved them from the flames
More desirable than gold, - sweeter than the hon-eycomb
Bless'd is He who loves – the fear of the Lord. Barekmor

+ Glory be to the Father, Son and Holy Spirit

Unto the ages of ages and for ever more.

I, Ephrem, am near-ing death - and I write my test-ament
Pray without ceasing – all day and all night
When the ploughman ploughs two times his harvest is- fruitful
Do not be like slothful ones, whose fields sprout up–with thorns
May this be a witness to
My disciples after me:
For he who loves it receives – great reward in both the worlds
Pray without ceasing – all day and all night

Lord have mercy upon us and help us.

BO'UTHO of MOR EPHREM

(Tone 7)

Lord, have mercy upon us
O Lord, receive our service
Send us from Your treasure-house
Mercy, grace and forgiveness

By our unpleasing actions,
We have angered You, O Lord
You are full of compassion
And Your peace is not disturbed

Ocean of mercy, You are –
Our sins are a drop of mud
And a drop of mud cannot
Make a vast ocean muddy

Glory be to Your great love
Which is shed upon sinners
Honor to Your Father and
To the Holy Spirit, praise

Lord who hearkens to our pray'rs
Unto us be reconciled
Hear our pray'r and petitions
Answer us in Your mercy

Kurielaison, Kurielaison, Kurielaison

*Turn to **Psalms of Compline (p. 10)***

NIGHT VIGIL of DAY FOUR (Wednesday)

Qaumo (p.5)...Introductory Prayer (p.13)... Psalms of Night (p.13)

ENIYONO

(Iro d'lo Domekh/Unarverum naadha...)

You who do not sleep - awaken me to repent

By night, with watchers - let us give thanks and sing praise

O holy virgin - may your pray'r be our stronghold

O The`o`tokos - may your pray'r be our stronghold

Prophets! Apostles! - may your pray'r be our stronghold

Martyrs! Confessors! - may your pray'r be our stronghold

Fathers and doctors - may your pray'r be our stronghold

You monks and hermits - may your pray'r be our stronghold

Have mercy on me - by Your grace, Son of the Good

Lord, You give repose, - to the faithful departed...*Barekmor*

+ Glory be to the Father, Son and the Holy Spirit
Unto to the ages of ages and forever more.

Praise and thanksgiving - we offer the Trinity

Kurieleison, Kurieleison, Kurieleison

Turn to the ***Introductory Prayer of 1st Qaumo (p. 14)***

1st QAUMO

EQBO

(Abo k'thab wo)

The Father wrote a letter - and sent it to Nazareth
To Virgin Mary - in whom he was pleased
That she should bear His own Son - who comes to redeem the world

Lord have mercy; Lord have mercy, Lord have mercy
(Kurieleison, Kurieleison, Kurieleison)

Lord, have mercy upon us
Lord, be kind and have mercy
Answer, Lord, and have mercy

Glory be to You, O Lord
Glory be to You, O Lord
Glory be to You, our hope forever. *Barekmor*

QOLO
(Bkhul Medem)

The Virgin bore a wonder – let us go and contemplate
The Ancient of Days – wrapped in swaddling clothes
The virgin bore an elder, the Ancient of Days
He who holds mountains is carried by a maiden
He gives bread to the hungry
But is nursed like an infant
The Son with no beginning – willed to have a beginning
He came to birth and – He is without end. Barekmor

+ Glory be to the Father, Son and the Holy Spirit
Unto to the ages of ages and forevermore.

The just of old gave fair names – to the daughter of David,
The holy virgin; – the bless`ed Mary;
Exiled prophet Ezek'iel called her the closed door;
Solomon, the enclosed garden and sealed fountain;
David called her a city
Where a seedless herb sprouted
Our Lord has become the food – of all the nations of earth
And magnifies her – in heav'n and on earth

Lord have mercy upon us and help us

BO'UTHO of MOR JACOB

O bless`ed one, may your pray'rs be with us always
May the Lord hear your pray'rs and have mercy on us

A watcher descended when Mary was at pray'r
And gave to her the greeting of peace sent by God

The *fiery* one said to her, "Peace be unto you
You shall conceive a son in your virginity."

The watcher said, "Be not troubled, full of beauty,
The Lord is pleased that you should bear His only Son

Behold, you shall receive a wond'rous conception
And shall bring forth a child whose kingdom has no end

By the pray'r of her who carried you for nine months
O Son of God, remove from us the scourge of wrath

*Turn to the **Praise of the Cherubim (p. 14)***

2nd QAUMO

*Turn to **Introductory Prayer of 2nd Qaumo (p. 15)***

EQBO

(Abo k'thab wo)

Bless`ed is He who made you – healing springs flowing on earth
He made His pow`er – abide in your bones
Elect and holy martyrs – pray to your Lord for our sake

Lord have mercy, Lord have mercy, Lord have mercy
(Kurieleison, Kurieleison, Kurieleison)

Lord, have mercy upon us
Lord, be kind and have mercy
Answer, Lord, and have mercy

Glory be to You, O Lord
Glory be to You, O Lord
Glory be to You, our hope forever. *Barekmor*

QOLO

(Bkhul Medem)

You righteous who loved the truth; –you just who died for His love
Your mem`o`ry is – a blessing for us
You harbors of relief for sinners who repent,
Pray with us to Christ who rests in your holy bones
That He may show compassion
And be merciful to us
And grant us unveiled faces – at the throne of His Godhead
And we will sing praise – by night and by day. *Barekmor*

+ Glory be to the Father, Son and the Holy Spirit
Unto to the ages of ages and forevermore.

Fair and lovely was the word - our Lord spoke in His gospel
He declared bless`ed - the zealous faithful
    "Bless'd are the poor in spirit, theirs is the kingdom;
    Bless'd are those who mourn for they shall be comforted;"
        Bless'd are the persecuted
        And the martyrs who were slain
For the suff'rings which they bore- and the pain which they endured
The kingdom is theirs- and eternal life.

Lord have have mercy upon us and help us.

BO'UTHO of MOR EPHREM

Lord, have mercy upon us
By the pray'rs of Your servants
By their pray'rs and petitions
Have mercy upon our souls

    May prophets who spoke of You,
    The apostles who preached You,
    And martyrs who died for You
    Intercede with You for us

Make mem'ry, Lord and Savior
Of the prophets, apostles
The martyrs, and the righteous
And help us by their pray`ers

    Pray for us, O holy ones
    To the One whose will you did
    That He may withdraw from us
    The scourge and the rod of wrath

Glory be to the Strong One
To Him who strengthened you all,
Prophets, apostles, *and* martyrs
Who won vict'ry by the Cross

    Lord have mercy upon us
    By the pray'rs of Your servants
    By their pray'rs and petitions
    Have mercy upon our souls

Turn to the ***Praise of the Cherubim (p. 15)***

3rd QAUMO

*Turn to **Introductory Prayer of 3rd Qaumo (p. 15)***

EQBO

(Abo k'thab wo)

Give rest to our departed – in Your glor`i`ous abodes
Lord, give rest to them – and mercy to us
While you forgive and blot out – the faults of us and of them

Lord have mercy, Lord have mercy, Lord have mercy
(Kurieleison, Kurieleison, Kurieleison)

Lord, have mercy upon us
Lord, be kind and have mercy
Answer, Lord, have mercy

Glory be to You, O Lord
Glory be to You, O Lord
Glory be to You, our hope forever. *Barekmor*

QOLO

(Bkhul Medem)

Grant rest, O Lord, unto them
Our fathers and our brethren – have departed from this life
'Til resurrection comes for those who sleep
Give rest, O Lord, to their souls in abodes of light
May their bones quicken on the day of their mem'ry
When Your command raises up
All the children of Adam
May they be clothed with glory, - enter the bridal chamber
And offer praises to You, their Savior. *Barekmor*

+ Glory be to the Father, Son and the Holy Spirit
Unto to the ages of ages and forevermore.

Bless`ed are the dead for whom – the living make off`e`rings
For their mem'ries are written in heaven
If Moses wrote the tribe's names on tables of stone
That they might have eternal mem'ry before God
Lord, on the Host full of life
Record the names of Your dead
That they may be remembered – in the Church and in heaven
And when the Lord comes they rejoice with him

Lord have mercy upon us and help us

BO'UTHO of MOR BALAI

Renew Your creatures by the res'rrection,
Your worshippers who have slept in Your hope.

Give rest and pardon to the dead, O Lord,
Who sleep in hope and await Your coming.

Lord, with Abraham, Isaac and Jacob,
Make Your servants rest, those who sleep in hope.

Their bodies and souls shall cry together:
"Bless'd is he who will come and raise the dead."

*Turn to **p. 16 to continue Night Vigil***

QOLO of the DAY

(Enono Nuhro)

Behold, Saint (Athanasius)
Your mem'ry is glor`i`ous
Angels rejoice in heaven
And the sons of men on earth
Your Lord rejoices in you
And beholds your hero`i`cs
Your Lord calls out unto you:
"Servant, enter the kingdom,
Which will never pass away." ...*Barekmor*

+ Glory be to the Father, Son and the Holy Spirit
Unto the ages of ages and forevermore.

Watchers rose and descended
To crown Mor (Philoxenos)
They proclaimed, "Bless`ed are you
Who have finished the contest"
Watchers in the heights rejoice
And await the sight of you
The Father and Son greet you
And the Holy Spirit weaves
A crown for your sacred head

Lord have mercy upon us and help us!

BO'UTHO of MOR EPHREM

Lord have mercy by the pray'rs
Of Your mother and the saints
By their pray'rs, Lord, have mercy
On us and upon our dead

May the angels who strengthened
The martyrs in the battle
Come and strengthen us against
The evil one and his pow'rs

May the angel who sprinkled
Dew on the three holy youths
Sprinkle the dew of mercy
On the bones of all the dead

Come, brethren, and offer praise
To the Holy Trinity
In memory of Mary,
The saints, and the departed

Lord have mercy by the pray'rs
Of Your mother and the saints
By their pray'rs, Lord, have mercy
On us and upon our dead

Turn to the ***Hymn of the Angels (p. 20)***

MATINS of DAY FOUR [Wednesday]

Qaumo (p. 5)... Introductory Prayer (p.21)... Psalms of Matins (p.21)

ENIYONO

(Am Bthultho/Nistayil ninne petta…)

With the Holy Virgin – who bore You in purity
Make us worthy – to sing praise to You, O Lord God

With the True Prophets who – prophesied of Your coming
Make us worthy – to sing praise to You, O Lord God

With Martyrs *and* Confessors – who endured torments and pain
Make us worthy – to sing praise to You, O Lord God

With Saint Basil the Great – and Noble Saint Gregory
Make us worthy – to sing praise to You, O Lord God

With the five wise virgins – who were ready with their lamps
Make us worthy – to sing praise to You, O Lord God

With the thief who believed – whom You promised Paradise
Make us worthy – to sing praise to You, O Lord God…*Barekmor*

+ Glory be to the Father, Son and Holy Spirit
Unto the ages of ages and forevermore.

With angels in heaven – who praise You unceasingly
Make us worthy – to sing praise to You, O Lord God

Turn to ***Psalm 113 (p. 23)***

EQBO

(Maryam diletokh/Nin jananee…)

May Mary who bore You – and John who baptized You
Intercede for us – O Lord, have mercy on us all
Stoumen Kalos, Kurielaison

QOLO

(l'Malkuth Rawmo/Krupa cheyaname, Nadha…)

Lord have mercy, have mercy on me
May this incense, which – we offer to You
Be for the pardon
And forgiveness of our sins.
Make us stand, O Living Son
At Your right hand on that day
When Your mercy manifests
O God, who – saved us by Your Cross. *Barekmor*

+ Glory be to the Father, Son and Holy Spirit
Unto the ages of ages and for ever more.

Glory to You, Lord, - who *being* Eternal-
With God the Father,
Low`ered Your great majesty
From the hidden heights above
And became man by Your will
And healed the diseases of
Adam's race. Glory to You Lord!

Theotokos

Mount Sinai trembled – at Your presence, Lord
Yet the Bless'd Virgin
Carried You, Lord, who carries
All of the heights and the depths
She conceived You without man
And brought You forth wondrously.
Magnify her mem'ry, O Lord

O Virgin Mary, - the angel brought you
This message of peace:
"In You shall dwell *the* King of kings"
Whom you will bear without man"
Bless'd are you bless`ed mother
For you brought forth the great Sun
Who gives light to all creation

Saints

Saints are invited – to the High Kingdom
Which ear has not heard
Nor has the eye of flesh seen
Nor the human heart conceived
That which God has prepared for
Those noble ones who loved Christ
Bless'd are those who are made worthy

The Martyrs proclaim: - "Our crown awaits us
And our reward is
Kept for us in His Kingdom
We suffered by *fire* and sword
So Christ will console us in
The Paradise He promised
To all those who truly love Him"

Repentance

Christ the King at Your – door of compassion
I knock ev'ry hour –
and from Your rich treasure-house
I ask for mercy and grace
In You Lord, I take refuge
Shame me not, I've confessed You
You're my hope - and strong protection

How narrow the door – and straight the path, which
Leads to the Kingdom
He who wants to follow it
Needs restraint and discipline
He who relaxes his guard
Is drawn to the path of sin
By his will – he will lose his soul

Departed

Those who are sealed in – holy baptism
With the seal of Christ
Who ate His Holy Body
And drank His Absolving Blood
Shall be raised up from the dust
To life eternal and shall
Be clothed in – garments of glory
Lord have mercy upon us and help us

QOLO

(Eno no nuhro/ Ruju mathikal irulil…)

Light has arisen in darkness for the righteous
At the time - when the light appears
And takes away the darkness
Heaven and - earth worship You, Lord
These two were made at one time:
One a firmament above
The other held the waters
And the air stretched between them,
A bridal chamber arose.–Praise to you, Lord, for Your works. *Barekmor*

+ Glory be to the Father, Son and Holy Spirit
Unto the ages of ages and for ever more.

Glory to - the Holy Father
Who sent forth His Holy Son
And He dwelt - in the holy womb
That we might become like Him
He became a son of man
In our image and likeness
That He might make us sons of
His Father and partakers - of His One Holy Spirit

Mother of God

While Mary - was standing in pray'r
The archangel, clothed in flame - came to her
And said "Peace to You
Palace in which the Prince dwells".
Your poverty was removed
When the Rich One descended
And entered into Your womb
So that He might satisfy - the hunger of the nations

Bless'd are you - Mary, who gave birth
To the living Son of God - Bless'd are you
Most precious vessel
In whom the merchant did dwell
Perfect palace who received
The architect of the heights
You bore Him in purity -
Bless`ed is the Lord who came - from you, O Virgin Mary

Saints

Our Lord said - "I am the True Light
And all those who walk in it; the darkness
Shall not overtake"
Bless`ed are the apostles
Who walked in the light of Christ.
May their pray'rs be a stronghold
And a refuge for our souls
May their mem'ries be honored - from end to end of the earth.

The martyrs - saw two paths ahead
One to life and one to death
And they yearned - for the narrow way
They descended to battle
And conquered the evil one
They ascended proclaiming:
"May the Lord's name be bless`ed
For He is the friend of those - who call on Him in their need"

Repentance

Lord be kind and have mercy
Lord, do not - withhold Your mercy
From sinners who call on You
And in Your - mercy save us from
Punishments and rods of wrath
Instead grant us months of joy
And years of Your abundance
By the great sign of Your Cross
Lord, cast down the enemy - that we may give thanks to You

I will not - cease praising You, Lord
Nor from singing hymns to You -
Lord, do not - bring me to judgement
For I know that I have sinned
And if you judge me justly
I'll inherit Gehenna
I shall be cut off from life
And unable to praise You. - Forgive me in Your mercy

Departed

Lord give rest – and remembrance to
Our fathers and brethren who
Have fallen – asleep in Your hope
    Lord, When You sit in Judgment
    To divide good from evil
    Place them in the ranks of saints
Let them behold Your mercy
When Your majesty appears.- Let them stand at Your right hand

PETHGOMO

(Tone 7 – Dhanikajanam kazhchayumaayarthikkum nin sampreethi)

The rich among the people \ shall seek your face with off`e`rings –
Halleluiah, Halleluiah
All the beauty of the king's daughter – is within

The virgins who are her companions shall follow after her –
Halleluiah, Halleluiah
They shall go in joy – and gladness…*Barekmor*

+ Glory be to the Father, Son and Holy Spirit
Unto the ages of ages and forevermore.

EQBO

(Shlom Lekh)

Peace to – you, Virgin pure and holy
Peace be with you, O pearl who is with-out stain
Who bore – the Almighty One who carries the whole cre-ation
All generations shall call you greatly bless`ed – forever
Stoumen Kalos, Kurieleison

QOLO

(Tubayk Idto/Karthavine vazhthum njanelaypozhum)

I will bless the Lord at all times and all seasons
Bless`ed is Christ – who chose you, Virgin Mary
From all the generations
He came and took flesh from you
As man He was subject to
The passions yet re-mained God
Praise to Him who so abased
His majesty for our sakes
And exalted His mother
In the four quarters of earth…*Barekmor*

+ Glory be to the Father, Son and Holy Spirit
Unto the ages of ages and forevermore.

Glory be to You, O God, the Word of life
Who of Your own will took flesh
Of the bless'd, virgin Mary
Who, in soul and in body
Was indeed pure and holy
She conceived without a man
And bore You in myst`ery
Instead of the seed of man
She conceived of the Spirit

Lord have mercy upon us and help us!

BO'UTHO of MOR JACOB

Make us share, Lord- in Your mother's –and saints' mem'ry
By their pray'rs have – mercy on us – and on our dead

Bless`ed are You – Mary for you – were prefigured
Myster'iously – by the ark, which – Moses fashioned
In the ark were – Tablets of Law –written by God
But, in You Ma-ry was the Bread – of Life in Truth

Bless`ed are the – dead who have slept – and rest in peace
The flesh of the – Son rests within – them as a pledge
He will cast down – the walls of She`ol for the dead,
They will hear His – voice and go with – haste to meet Him

Son born in the – flesh from the dau-ghter of David
Pour Your mercy – upon Your flock – in abundance

Turn to ***Concluding Prayer of Matins (p. 23)***

THIRD HOUR of DAY FOUR [Wednesday]

Qaumo (p. 5)

Introductory Prayer (p. 24)

QOLO

(Eno no Nuhro/Daivathe pettoru mathavam…)

Bless'd is - Mary the Mother
Who did bring forth God the Word
Upon her knees she carried
Him who is the lamb of God
She was not harmed by His light
Nor by fervor of His *fire*
For His strength supported her
She bore Him who was carried
By the Cherubim's chariot. *Barekmor*

+ Glory be to the Father, Son and Holy Spirit
Unto the ages of ages and for ever more.

By three – myst'ries, the Church does
Teach a lesson to doubters:
A tree, - a rock, and a fish
Which brought forth wond`e`rous fruit
The tree did bring forth a lamb
The rock did flow with water
The fish did bring forth a coin
These three – reprove him who doubts
The myst'ry of Virgin birth

Lord have mercy upon us and help us.

BO'UTHO of MOR JACOB

May your pray'r be with us always O Bless`ed One –
May the Lord hear your pray'rs and have mercy on us

With awe I speak of Mary, the earthly daughter
I wonder at the height to which she ascended

Grace made the Son descend to her; she found favor
As to become the Mother of the Son of God

In whom shall I dwell but in the meek and humble
He dwelt in her who was the most humble of all

For no one was ever so humble as Mary
And none was ever so exalted as she was

By the pray'rs of her who carried You for nine months
O Son of God remove from us the scourge of wrath

Qaumo (p. 5)

SIXTH HOUR of DAY FOUR [Wednesday]

Qaumo (p. 5)... Introductory Prayer (p. 25)

QOLO
(Thuro d'Seenai)

Peace to you Mary
Ark of Myst`eries
Which Moses fashioned
Veil of the Spirit, which the
Living waters prefigured
Peace to You, O strong city
Of which Prophet David spoke: -
God came forth - from your holy womb. *Barekmor*

+ Glory be to the Father, Son and Holy Spirit

The martyrs put on
The Cross as armor
And fought with Satan
Some were slaughtered by the sword
Some were burned by the fi`re
The evil one saw this and
was enraged for they triumphed
By their pray'r – O Lord have mercy

Unto the ages of ages and forever more.

At the table which –
You prepared for those
Just and righteous ones
Seat our departed who have
Consumed Your Body and Blood
In their lives they confessed You,
Confess them to Your Father
Those who died – and slept in Your hope

Lord have mercy upon us and help us.

Turn to ***Bo'utho of Mor Balai (p. 25)***

NINTH HOUR of DAY FOUR [Wednesday]

Qaumo (p. 5)…Introductory Prayer (p. 27)

QOLO

(Lomath Talmeen)[2]

As garments which clothe the flow`ers of the field
Are not woven by the hands of mortal man,
So the righteous ones in the resurrection
Shall be clothed in garb the Spirit has woven…*Barekmor*

+ Glory be to the Father, Son and the Holy Spirit
From ages unto ages and forevermore

Adam said: "I worship that voice, which called me
Among the trees and I was afraid of it;
It shall call me and my children on that day
And place me at the right hand of His Godhead.

Lord have mercy upon us and help us!

BO'UTHO of MOR BALAI

Renew Your creatures by the res'rrection,
Your worshippers who have slept in Your hope.

Give rest and pardon to the dead, O Lord,
Who sleep in hope and await Your coming.

Lord, with Abraham, Isaac and Jacob,
Make Your servants rest, those who sleep in hope.

Their bodies and souls shall cry together:
"Bless'd is He who will come and raise the dead

Qaumo (p. 5)

[2] The melodies are identical to the tones for *l'Maryam Yoldath Aloho*

VESPERS of DAY FIVE [Thursday]

Qaumo (p. 5)... Introductory Prayer (p. 8)... Psalms of Vespers (p. 8)

EQBO

(Shmayone Shub'ho/Vaazthunu vaanavar vaanil)

Those in heaven sing praises
Those on earth offer worship
To the One, eternal God,
The creator of the world. *Staumen Kalos Kurielaison*

QOLO

(Naadhanodunnatha naadathil praarthichu njaan)

I called upon the Lord with my voice; with my voice I besought the Lord
With cries of praise - I satisfied You
Because of - my offences and my sins I beseech You while I cry out:
"My Lord and God cast me not from Your presence
I show my penitence and - compunction of heart
O King - because of my many faults, Lord have mercy"...*Barekmor*

+ Glory be to the Father, Son and Holy Spirit
Unto the ages of ages and forevermore.

Pardon my sins - and forgive my faults
By Your grace - O God, full of mercy, do not leave me to the enemy
That I may not be entangled in his snare
And become a laughing stock - and a source of scorn
Christ, God - at Your door I have knocked have mercy on me

On the Theotokos

A Watcher was - sent from the Palace
Of heaven - to the daughter of David in Nazareth of Galilee
And he brought a message of peace and announced:
"The Lord is with you and He - shall come forth from you"
Christ, God - First-Born of the Father have mercy on us

"Peace be with you," - creation cries out
O Virgin - Mother of God, who is filled with the beauty of holiness
Pray for us to your Son who came forth from you
That the Lord of all may send - forgiveness of sins
On this - assembly, which celebrates your mem`o`ry

On the Saints

Peace be with the – builders of the faith
And pillars–of the Holy Church: the prophets, apostles, and the martyrs
Who endured torments for the sake of our Lord
Their souls followed after him – By their pray'rs for us
Christ God - as King David sang, "Have mercy upon us"

The martyrs saw – Christ hung on the Cross
And His side – opened up by the spear, and blood and water flowing from it
They hastened to encourage one another:
"Come, let us die for the Lord – as He died for us"
Christ God – by the pray'rs of Your martyrs, Lord, have mercy

On Repentance

Open the door – of Your mercy, Lord,
As You did–for the thief and pardon us like Simon, who had denied You
Accept our repentance like the publican
And like the sinful woman, - Lord, full of mercy,
For You – are pleased with penitents when they come to You

The Ninevites – trembled at the voice
Of Jonah – and took refuge in penance by watching, fasting, and pray`ing,
And by tears and groans, the sentence of judgment
Of which Jonah had pronounced – was fully annulled
Bless`ed – be the Merciful One who turned them to good

On the Departed

Make mem'ry Lord – of the departed
Those faithful, – who consumed Your Holy Body and drank Your Atoning Blood
When You come in glory with all Your angels
May they stand at Your right hand – with faces unveiled
Christ, God – and may they offer praises to Your Godhead

Christ, sea of help –and full of mercy
Who came down – to the dwelling of the dead and proclaimed life to those on earth
And was raised up in glory on the third day
On the day of Your judgment – May Your servants be
Raised up – and take them to the bridal-chamber of joy

Lord have mercy upon us and help us

QOLO

(Saadharamethum nin bhavane en nercha ninakku kazhikum njaan Hal…)

In reverence will I enter your house and offer my vows to you Halleluiah
In the evening we - have come to Your house
Lord, to ask for mercy, grace, and forgiveness
In the morning may - we come worship You
Our Savior, for You have mercy on sinners…*Barekmor*

+ Glory be to the Father, Son and Holy Spirit
Unto the ages of ages and forevermore.

Praise to You, Watcher - whom the watchers serve
Who takes joy in the service of those on earth
As Jonah called You - from within the sea
From the depths we call upon You, hear our voice

On the Theotokos

Bless'd one who became - mother of God in
Purity and holiness as a virgin
Beg for mercy that - it may bring rest to
The departed and bring hope to the living

Mary was a ship - of life in the world
Christ was the captain who came and dwelt in her
She came and reached the - harbor of joy and
Gave heav`enly riches to the sons of men

On the Saints

O Holy Ones, may - peace be where you dwell
O, Merchants who brought life to the sons of men
Open to us your - treas`ury of pray'rs
And keep this place in which you dwell from all harm

As Noah, the just - preserved animals
Which entered with him on the day of the flood
Rise up, you martyrs, - protect creation
From the tempest and the waves, which surround it

On One Saint

Those on high marvel - those below honor
Your great name and your splendor, O St. (Thomas)
Your Lord, when He saw - the way of your life
Magnified your mem'ry, may your pray'r help us

On Repentance

O God who is pure - and who loves the pure
Grant purity of heart to us at all times
Remove from us all - vain concerns and thoughts
And cares that are not pleasing to You, O Lord

God who had pity - on Nineveh have
Pity on our generation, which has sinned
If You close Your door - O, Merciful One,
Where shall we go to knock, if not at Your door?

On the Departed

Raise the dead who have - received Your Body
And drank the cup of salvation of Your Blood
Raise them from the grave - without corruption
And clothe those who wait for You with Your glory

As the flow`ers of - the field are clothed in
Garments not woven by the hands of mankind
The just shall be clothed - in garments woven
By the Holy Spirit at Resurrection

PETHGOMO

(Tone 5/ En praarthana naadha kelkename Haleluiah)

O Lord, hear my pray'r - Halle-lu-iah
And may my cry come before You

For my days are consumed in smoke - Halle-lu-iah
And my bones are white as if they were burned...*Barekmor*

+ Glory be to the Father, Son and Holy Spirit
Unto the ages of ages and forevermore.

EQBO

(Brikh Dhadi/ Njangale nal nilamaakaname)

By Your compassion make us - like the fertile earth
And grow in our souls the seed - of Your commandments.
Stoumen Kalos Kurielaison

QOLO

(Mshalem Nuhre/ Bahumohanamathikamaneeyam)

How good and how lovely
The light of day is ending
Bring Your grace to completion
Remove from us the devil
Who lays snares for us always
May Your Cross be – our guard and our protection
By night and by day...*Barekmor*

+ Glory be to the Father, Son and Holy Spirit
Unto the ages of ages and forevermore.

Job cried out from the dunghill;
Daniel cried out from the den;
The three young men cried out from
The furnace and You saved them
Like them we cry – "O Lord, have mercy on us,
Who are poor sinners!"

Lord have mercy upon us and help us

BO'UTHO of MOR JACOB

O Lord – our Lord, we call – upon You to – come to our aid –
And hear our pleas – have mercy on – our souls!

O Lord, - pity me and – I will live by – your mercy that –
In Geh`enna – I not suffer – like the rich man. –
May baptism – spread its wings o'er – the flames and save –
Me from burning. – While I pass by – let me –

Not beg – as the rich man- begged for water –
From Abraham, - where it is known – that he who asks –
Will not receive. – Deliver me – from the torments –
Of the rich man – that along with – poor Lazarus – I praise

You Christ, - who has all the – authority –
Of the Kingdom – and Gehenna – Save us and have – mercy!

*Turn to **Concluding Prayer of Vespers (p. 9)***

COMPLINE of DAY FIVE (Thursday)

Qaumo (p. 5)... Introductory Prayer (p.10)

QOLO

(l'Maryam Yoldath Aloho/ En kaarthave kopathaal shasikaruthe)

Let him who comes to the holy place to pray
Cleanse his body and his soul from in`i`quity
Then the Lord will hear his pray'rs and petitions
And have mercy on him on the day of judgment...*Barekmor*

+ Glory be to the Father, Son and Holy Spirit
Unto the ages of ages and forevermore.

Let us wash our clothes with the tears of our eyes
For the coming of the Son of God is nearing
The world's end is at the door, as St. Paul spoke
Bless`ed is he whose judgment shall be with mercy

Lord have mercy upon us and help us

BO'UTHO of MOR JACOB

O Lord, our Lord, we call to You come to our aid
Hear our requests and have mercy upon our souls

How lovely is the pray'r, which the Son of God taught
Bless'd is he who meditates on it and keeps it
All the beauty of justice and perfection is
Found there for him who takes pains to make it his pray'r

He taught you to pray 'Forgive me my debts and sins'
He desires to forgive and so He taught this pray'r
If the face of God were not turned t'wards forgiveness
He would not have taught us to say, "Forgive us, Lord"

O Lord, who hears all and who accepts earnest pray'rs
Hear our petition and have mercy on our souls

Kurielaison, Kurielaison, Kurielaison

*Turn to **Psalms of Compline (p. 10)***

NIGHT VIGIL on DAY FIVE (Thursday)

Qaumo (p.5)... Introductory Prayer (p.13)... Psalms of Night (p.13)

ENIYONO

(Aathmaave nee sthuthiyekaal)

Why is it that you love sleep
More than praising, O my soul?
How long will you be engrossed
In pleasures which profit not?
Awake now and rise and sing:
Lord of all, to you the praise

Now is the time to repent
Let every man turn from sin
Before the time passes and
There is no place to repent
Do not regard our misdeeds
Lord of all, to you the praise

"Forgive me, O forgive me"
The sinful woman cried out
And our Lord answered and said:
"Go your sins are forgiven
And your faults are blotted out"
Lord of all, to you the praise

Rebuke us not in anger
For we cannot bear it, Lord
Punish us not in your wrath
We will not stand before you
Do not regard our misdeeds
Lord of all, to you the praise

Pardon and forgive the sins
Of our fathers and brethren
Write them in the book of life,
They who have gone to their rest
Let them stand at your right hand
When your majesty appears ...*Barekmor*

+ Glory be to the Father, Son and Holy Spirit
Unto the ages of ages and forevermore.

Praise to the one who is three
And to the three who are one;
To the Father, and the Son,
And to the Holy Spirit.
Praise be to the one true God
And to us mercy always
Kurieleison, Kurieleison, Kurieleison

*Turn to the **Introductory Prayer of 1st Qaumo (p. 14)***

1st QAUMO

EQBO

(Faradaiso)

Your myst`ery, O daughter of David
Is prefigured by the ark of Noah
Prophecy has symbolized your image
And it has likened you to the new jar
Your son is the salt which seasoned the earth
And by it lives the whole world which was lost

Lord have mercy; Lord have mercy, Lord have mercy
(Kurieleison, Kurieleison, Kurieleison)

Lord, have mercy upon us
Lord, be kind and have mercy
Answer, Lord, and have mercy

Glory be to You, O Lord
Glory be to You, O Lord
Glory be to You, our hope forever. *Barekmor*

QOLO

(Moriyo Moran)

O Lord, our Lord
When Your Godhead was moved to– descend and clothe– itself in our flesh
Gabr`i`el flew
And carried the peace of God – and sowed it in – the ear of Mary:
"Peace be with you
The Lord is with you and the – Savior of all – shall come forth from you
Halleluiah
He is the King whose kingdom – shall have no end – unto the ages…*Barekmor*

+ Glory be to the Father, Son and Holy Spirit
Unto the ages of ages and forevermore.

Mary asked Christ

After she had brought him forth: - "I know not what - to call you my son.

You are a child

But you are older than time - The Ancient One - yet you are a child

I will call you

The splendor which shone forth from - the Father and - gave light to the world"

Halleluiah

Bless`ed are you and worship - to your Father - who sent you for us

Lord have mercy upon us and help us!

BOU'THO of MOR JACOB

O bless`ed one, may your pray'rs be with us always
May the Lord hear your pray'rs and have mercy on us

Come in peace, O you ship, which carried the new life;
Peace be with you, O palace in which the king dwelt,
O garden, in which was the branch of righteousness;
Peace be with you in whom the mystr'ies were preserved

Come in peace, fair among women and beautiful
Peace to you, veil which is spread over creation
Come in peace, O innocence which is undefiled
Peace be with you, Eve who brought forth Emman'u'el

By the pray'r of her who carried you for nine months
O Son of God, remove from us the scourge of wrath

Turn to the ***Praise of the Cherubim (p. 14)***

2nd QAUMO

Turn to the ***Introductory Prayer of 2nd Qaumo (p. 15)***

EQBO
(Faradaiso)

There are twelve pillars which carry the earth
There are also twelve months which crown the year
There are twelve springs which flowed in the desert
And twelve apostles who preached the gospel
They preached the gospel in the heights and depths
May their pray'r be our stronghold and refuge

Lord have mercy; Lord have mercy, Lord have mercy
(Kurieleison, Kurieleison, Kurieleison)

Lord, have mercy upon us
Lord, be kind and have mercy
Answer, Lord, and have mercy

Glory be to You, O Lord
Glory be to You, O Lord
Glory be to You, our hope forever. *Barekmor*

QOLO
(Moriyo Moran)

O Lord, our Lord
Like bright lamps the apostles - made disciples - of all the nations
And turned them all
Who were in captivity - to the devil - to the way of truth
They were baptized
In the name of the Father - and the Son and - the Holy Spirit...*Barekmor*

+ Glory be to the Father, Son and Holy Spirit
Unto the ages of ages and forevermore.

O Lord, our Lord
I entered the arena - of the martyrs - and saw their judgment
The flesh is burnt,
The body torn asunder - but the spirit - is glad and joyous
They cry and say:
"For your sake, Lord, we shall die - come to our help - and save us, Jesus"
Lord have mercy upon us and help us!

BO'UTHO of MOR EPHREM

Lord have mercy upon us
By the pray'rs of your servants
By their pray'rs and petitions
Have mercy upon our souls

'You have entered within me,'
The Church told the apostles
'You made me the King's daughter
Who is honored by princes'

Praise to Him who at two feasts
Granted His gifts to the Twelve
At one, His Body and Blood
At the other, the Spirit

Lord have mercy upon us
By the pray'rs of your servants
By their pray'rs and petitions
Have mercy upon our souls

*Turn to the **Praise of the Cherubim** (p. 15)*

3rd QAUMO

*Turn to **Introductory Prayer of 3rd Qaumo (p. 15)***

EQBO
(Faradaiso)

Jesus, Son of the Father, be our help
O Jesus, Son of Mary, protect us
O Jesus, give strength to us and guard us
Jesus, drive out the evil one from us
Jesus, forgive our offenses and sins
O Jesus, have mercy when you judge us

Lord have mercy; Lord have mercy, Lord have mercy
(Kurieleison, Kurieleison, Kurieleison)

Lord, have mercy upon us
Lord, be kind and have mercy
Answer, Lord, have mercy
Glory be to You, O Lord
Glory be to You, O Lord
Glory be to You, our hope forever. *Barekmor*

QOLO
(Akfirmo)

The Lord shall free the captives, Halleluiah
At night Simon Peter went forth from prison
At night the shackles fell from the hands of Paul
And at night do you cut off – the fetters and our bonds of sin

+ Glory be to the Father, Son and Holy Spirit
Unto the ages of ages and forevermore.

At night a star of light appeared to Jacob
At night, a pillar of light stood ov'r Isr`a`el
And at night let your light shine – in the hearts of your worshippers

Lord have mercy upon us and help us!

BO'UTHO of MOR BALAI

Renew Your creatures by the res'rrection,
Your worshippers who have slept in Your hope.

Give rest and pardon to the dead, O Lord,
Who sleep in hope and await Your coming.

Lord, with Abraham, Isaac and Jacob,
Make Your servants rest, those who sleep in hope.

Their bodies and souls shall cry together:
"Bless'd is He who will come and raise the dead."

Turn to ***p. 16 to continue Night Vigil***

QOLO of the DAY

(Lomath Thalmeen)

How lovely is your festival St. (Balai)
It is like April, all adorned with flow`ers
April makes the earth rejoice with its flow`ers
Your mem'ry gives us joy and we seek your pray'rs...*Barekmor*

+ Glory be to the Father, Son and Holy Spirit
Unto the ages of ages and forevermore.

Bless'd is the mother who bore you, St. (Sarah);
How fair the tree which she planted in Eden
With its root in the earth and its head in heav'n
Its fruit gives help to all who are afflicted
Lord have mercy upon us and help us!

BO'UTHO of MOR JACOB

May your pray'r be with us, O bishops and fathers
May the Lord hear your pray'rs and have mercy on us

The bishops, who taught the faith, preached according to
The words taught by Simon Peter without dispute
They trod in the footsteps of their masters and walked
In the way of the apostles without stumbling

Saints Matthew, Mark, and along with them, Luke and John,
The evangelists, drank from the source of Eden
Through them, it flowed forth as a doctrine full of life
They went and quenched the thirsty earth with their doctrine

By your pray'rs may the Lord remove the scourge of wrath
From all people who take refuge in you with faith

Turn to the ***Hymn of the Angels (p. 20)***

MATINS of DAY FIVE (Thursday)

Qaumo (p.5)...Introductory Prayer (p.21)...Psalms of Matins (p.21)

ENIYONO

(Mumberai thirumumbil...)

I – come – before You
And I pray and beseech You to for-give-my – offences –
You are a merciful God
O Lord, - have compassion and mercy

There – is- no other
Sinner like me on this earth who has-sinned-and- angered You
By my pray'r I appease You
O Lord, - have compassion and mercy

I – sink – in my sins,
In the multitude of them, as in-a-sea, - Lord of all
Draw me from them by Your grace
O Lord, - have compassion and mercy

From – my – mother's womb
You have always been my God "Do not-leave-me,' – sang David
'O Lord, do not rebuke me'
O Lord, - have compassion and mercy

I am like – that servant
"Who did not use the talent his Lord-en-trus-ted to him"
Count me with him who had ten
O Lord, - have compassion and mercy

I am like – that fig tree
Which did not bring forth its fruit; You ord-ered-it – be cut down
Fruit, who came forth from Mary
O Lord, - have compassion and mercy

Lord, - my - offences
And my faults overwhelm me I be-seech-you, - O Kind One
Pardon them, Lord, by Your grace
O Lord, - have compassion and mercy...*Barekmor*

+ Glory be to the Father, Son and Holy Spirit
Unto the ages of ages and forevermore.

The – pow'rs - of heaven
Sing glory and praise to You and we,-on-earth, - sing with them
We sing praise to Your Godhead
O Lord, - have compassion and mercy. Amin.

*Turn to **Psalm 113 (p. 23)***

EQBO

(Aloho adarain/Udayone thunacheyka…)

God, save me – for the storms
And tempests – of the sins
Which I have – committed - surround me
Be a harbor of peace, Lord
That I may – not be drowned in sin
I seek to repent, stretch out Your hand
As You did to Peter- and have mercy
Upon me, O Lord!
Stoumen Kalos, Kurieleison

QOLO

(Thal praarthana njangalkabayam – Pauranikanam…)

May your prayers be our stronghold
O prophets, apostles, and holy martyrs
You are sweet incense
For on you the Holy Church is built in faith
Intercede for her children who seek refuge
From your holy bones…*Barekmor*

+ Glory be to the Father, Son and Holy Spirit
Unto the ages of ages and forevermore.

Every morning praise Him who by a gesture
Rules the creation
He fills earth and heav'n, which are too small for Him
But the hearts of the righteous are large enough
Bless'd are those who pray

On the Theotokos

O Solomon, fair child, what is that garden
Of which you did sing
Which was closed and sealed in its virginity?
"It is Mary from whom came forth the gard'ner
Who sowed Paradise."

The door, which Ezek'iel saw prefigured You
O holy virgin
Man never entered it, but only the Lord
Praise to Him who humbled Himself for Adam
To restore his race

On the Saints

In the morning, the Son went to find help for
His Father's vineyard
He *hired* first the prophets and the apostles
And the thief at the e`leventh *hour* and sent
Him to Paradise

Our Lord said to the saints, who hated this world
And all its pleasures
"Bless`ed are you for whom there is kept on high
The garden, the table of the Kingdom and
The marriage-chamber"

On the Morning

At morning, the merchants of Mid`i`an drew
Joseph from the pit.
They paid the price for the young son of Rachel
And they took him from there and went to Egypt
Where he became king

On Repentance

I knock at Your door and I beg for mercy
From Your treasure-house
I am a sinner who has strayed from Your way
Grant that I confess and be free from my sins
And live in Your grace

Where shall we go to knock, if not at Your door?
Compassionate Lord?
O King, whom the kings of the earth give honor
If Your mercy does not plead, who will be there
To plead for our faults?

On the Departed

Good one, full of mercy, judge not Your servants
Who have worshipped You
And with them, do not enter into judgment
For no man living is justified before
The dread judgment-seat

O Lord, make the departed, bought by the blood,
Which flowed from Your side,
To rest in the bosom of Abraham and
Clothe them with glory and give them joy with You
In Your Father's house

Lord have mercy upon us and help us!

QOLO

(Moran yeshu mshiho – Udaye kadalinnudayone...)

Our Lord Jesus Christ
At morning, churches sing praise
The monasteries rejoice
At morning the tongues of beasts and birds make a joyful noise
And the sea worships You with
The islands and their dwellers...*Barekmor*

+ Glory be to the Father, Son and Holy Spirit
Unto the ages of ages and forevermore.

At morning, the Church gives thanks
Which You made like Paradise
But instead of trees and plants it is filled with souls of men
And on the harp of David
She sings praise to the bridegroom

On the Theotokos

He who makes rain pour from clouds
And sprinkles earth with show`ers
Was nursed with the drops of milk from the breast of the Virgin
And wonder filled His Mother
When she bore and carried Him

He is lulled like a baby
The infant older than time
Behold, the One before whom John leapt now leaps like a *child*
And the Ancient of Days is
Carried in the Virgin's arms

On the Saints

Peace be with all the prophets
Peace be with the apostles
And peace be with the martyrs who loved the Lord God of peace
Peace be with the Holy Church
In which the sons of peace dwell

Martyrs, who did not offer
Incense before vain idols
Behold, the sweet scent of your death is fragrant like spices
Kings raise their crowns and worship
Before your holy relics

On One Saint

We shall see you, St. (Thomas)
Standing with an unveiled face
Before Christ saying, "These are the sheep you entrusted me
Acknowledge to Your Father
Those who have confessed You, Lord"

On the Morning

In the morning, Shamouni
Offered up her prayr's to God:
"O God, give judgment for me before King Anti`o`chus
He slays my sons like sheep and
Charges me like a lion"

Shamouni said to the king,
"Of my seven noble sons,
I will not give even one to you to serve as a slave
I will give them to the Lord
Because they are His servants"

On Repentance

God, who is rich in mercy,
Answer sinners who call You,
For we know that we have sinned O Lord, we knock at Your door
Bring forth from Your treasure-house
Pardon of our offences

Sinner, come beg for mercy
The door of God is open
And He will grant your requests; do not delay repentance
For you do not know the time
When the angel of death comes

On the Departed

On altars throughout the earth
Make good mem'ry, O Savior
Of all those who ate your Flesh and Blood and confessed You, Lord
Keep the living by Your Cross
And pardon the departed

When the sea of fi`re roars
And consumes the imp`i`ous,
By the sweet sound of Your living voice, - raise our departed
Who have rested in Your hope
And confessed the Trinity

PETHGOMO

(Tone 1/ En aathmavine ninkaluyarthunen naadha)

I lift up my soul to You, O Lord – Halleluiah w`Halleluiah
In You I trust, do not let me be – put to shame

Let the wicked be ashamed in their vanity–Halleluiah w`Halleluiah
Show me Your paths, - O my Lord…*Barekmor*

+ Glory be to the Father, Son and Holy Spirit
Unto the ages of ages and forevermore.

EQBO

(Mor Ephrem/ Prabha nine vandhikunnu)

The light, O Lord, worships You
Those in heaven praise Your name
All creation worships You
At dawn when Your light – a-ppears …*Stoumen Kalos, Kurieleison*

QOLO

(B'safro Hazawuy/Udayathinkalunarnarnapol)

At morning, Jacob the just
Was awakened from his sleep
He mar-velled at the ladder
Which the – angels ascended
Which was set upon the earth
And reached up to the heavens…*Barekmor*

+ Glory be to the Father, Son and Holy Spirit
Unto the ages of ages and forevermore.

At morning, Simon Peter
Walked on the sea before Christ
And when – his mind wavered he
Began – to sink in the waves
And the Lord reached out His hand
And drew him from sea to land

Lord have mercy upon us and help us!

BO'UTHO of MOR JACOB

Open – unto us, - your great door – full of me-rcy,
Lord, hear – our pray'r and – have mercy – upon our – souls

The Lord – loves pray'r made – in secret – in the in-ner
Chamber – for the just – did not tri-umph with loud – cries
By the – pray'r and hu-mility – of Moses,
Isr`a`el- crossed the sea- but Pharoah –drowned in his – pride

God heard – the pray'r of – David and – had mercy – on
Him and – restored to – him the gift – of prophe-cy
Inside – the furnace – the three youths – called upon – God
And He – delivered – them from the – consuming flames

My Lord- three things make – me tremble – and frighten – me
Namely, - Death, the dread – judgment seat, - and Gehenna

Turn to ***Concluding Prayer of Matins (p. 23)***

THIRD HOUR of DAY FIVE [Thursday]

Qaumo (p. 5)... Introductory Prayer (p. 24)

QOLO

(Moriyo Moran)

Woe be to me – I was a slave to evil,
 And ignored death – like a crim`i`nal;
Trampling the law, – I rose against Your commands
 My evil will – became law for me;
Now I have lost – the garments of virtue and
 I am naked, – Lord, save me from death.... *Barekmor*

+ Glory be to the Father, Son and Holy Spirit
Unto the ages of ages and forevermore.

Woe be to him – whose soul is bound to this world,
 Because that bond – cannot be broken
The world deceives; – he who loves it cannot be
 Diligent for – it is seductive
Bless'd is he who – like a diligent merchant,
 Has acquir`ed – life which shall not end

Lord have mercy upon us and help us!

BO'UTHO of MOR JACOB

O Lord, our Lord, we call to You, come to our aid;
Hear our requests and have mercy upon our souls.

 I long for Your pardon that it may come to me;
 Give me tears to beg for mercy while I have time;
 When the day ends, the shadows of death surround me;
 Be to me, O Lord, a sun; let me see Your light;

Let me not confront my death outside Your vineyard;
O Good One, accept the *hour* of my repentance.
My end has come while I have labored at vain things
At the end of my life, grant that I may be Yours

 Answer, O Lord! Answer, O Lord! And have mercy!
 Turn the hearts of the sons of men to repentance.

Qaumo (p. 5)

SIXTH HOUR of DAY FIVE [Thursday]

Qaumo (p. 5)…Introductory Prayer (p. 25)

QOLO

(B'safro Hazawuy/Shlomo d'abo/ Deivathin maathaavaayol…)

By Bless'd Mary the myst'ries
Of the prophets were fulfilled:
  The bush, the urn, the manna,
  And Aaron's staff, which budded
May her pray'r be our refuge,
Both on earth and in heaven…*Barekmor*

+ Glory be to the Father, Son and Holy Spirit

By the pray'r of the prophets,
The apostles and martyrs,
  Holy fathers and doctors,
  Of the true orthodox faith
Make peace and tranquility
Dwell throughout the creation.

Unto the ages of ages and forevermore.

May the dead who have decayed
And become dust of the earth
  Be roused from sleep by Your voice
  From the grave to Paradise
And with the just and righteous,
Inherit eternal life

Lord have mercy upon us and help us!

Turn to ***Bo'utho of Mor Balai (p. 25)***

NINTH HOUR of DAY FIVE (Thursday)

Qaumo (p. 5)…Introductory Prayer (p. 27)

QOLO

(Barubto Brishith/ Puthranilettu paran…)[3]

Paul has written us – "Those who died in Christ
Shall never taste death;
Even though they sleep – life has called to them;
How greatly bless'd are
Halleluiah w`Halleluiah,
Those who sleep in Christ…*Barekmor*

+ Glory be to the Father, Son and Holy Spirit
Unto the ages of ages and forevermore.

I passed by a tomb, - and contemplated
The way of the world;
The slave and his lord – are equal in death;
While kings who now sleep,
Halleluiah w`Halleluiah,
Have lost their pow`er.
Lord have mercy upon us and help us!

BO'UTHO of MOR BALAI

Renew Your creatures by the res'rrection,
Your worshippers who have slept in Your hope.

Give rest and pardon to the dead, O Lord,
Who sleep in hope and await Your coming.

Lord, with Abraham, Isaac and Jacob,
Make Your servants rest, those who sleep in hope.

Their bodies and souls shall cry together:
"Bless'd is He who will come and raise the dead

Qaumo (p. 5)

VESPERS of DAY SIX [Friday]

Qaumo (p. 5)…Introductory Prayer (p. 8)…Psalms of Vespers (p. 8)

EQBO

(Haw Dat'ayn Kul/Ahkilandatha Vahippone)

He who bears all creation
Was borne by the wood – of the Cross
The living One who gives life
Tasted death of – His own will
The he-ro who cannot be
Held by – the ends of the earth
Nor contained by creation
Was contained within a tomb…*Staumen Kalos Kurielaison*

QOLO

(Bthultho Maryam/ Nin praarthana njangalkabhayam…)

May your pray'r be a stronghold for us
Glo-ry- be- to the Father; worship to the Son;
Thanksgiving to the Spirit
Bless'd –Tri-ni-ty three persons, three names, one true God
Unto Him belongs glory…*Barekmor*

+ Glory be to the Father, Son and Holy Spirit
Unto the ages of ages and forevermore.

All – cre-a-tion shall declare Your glory, O Christ
Who is the true King of kings
An-gels – and – men whom You created for Your praise
Sing to You by night and day

On the Theotokos

On – the – day – we remember the Virgin Mary
All creation rejoices
It – sings – praise – to the Lord who chose and magnified
The day of her remembrance

Like – the – sun – which descends and rests within the grape
And mixes sweetness in it
So – the – Word – came and rested in the virgin's womb
And came forth and redeemed us

On the Saints

Mar-tyrs – say – to their persecutors: "We fear not
The *fire* or the sharpened sword
If – the – flesh – dies the soul shall live on and sing praise
And thanksgiving to the Lord"

Mar-tyrs – were – slain for their Lord and their Lord was slain
To save Adam and his kin
Bless-`ed – is – He who by His death redeemed the Church
And she sings praises to Him

On Repentance

If – a-ny-one gains this world and loses his soul
His gain profits him nothing
Grant – us -, O – Lord to hate the world and gain our souls
And receive eternal life

"Go – in – peace –", said our Lord to the sinful woman,
"Your sins have been forgiven!
Tru-ly -! Tru-ly! Your penance will be remembered
When this Gospel is proclaimed."

On the Departed

Give – rest, - O – Lord, to Your servants in that kingdom,
Which shall never pass away
Write – their – names – in the Book of Life, which is above
In the heavenly Zi`on

No – one -; nei-ther father, nor mother, nor brethren
Can save us upon our death
But – Christ – will- raise the dead from their graves and never
Leave those who dwell in the tomb
Lord have mercy upon us and help us!

QOLO

(Barubto Brisith/ Shrushtichen mel nin kaivachu…)

You created me and placed Your hands upon me
In the beginning – on Friday, God created
Adam from – dust and breathed on him
And gave him speech that he might sing prai-ses
Hallelu-iah w'Ha-lleluiah, to his – creator… *Barekmor*

+ *Glory be to the Father, Son and Holy Spirit*
Unto the ages of ages and forevermore.

Praise to the Strong One, - who descended from the heights
And by His - Cross redeemed us all
And delivered us from sin and taught - us
Hallelu-iah w'Ha-lleluiah , to hon-or the Cross

On the Theotokos

Mary and E`lizabeth -were wondrous ships who sailed in
To harbor - one brought the preacher
And Mary bore the Savior of the - world
Hallelu-iah w'Ha-lleluiah, may their - pray'rs help us

Not among virgins - nor among the genera-tions of old
Nor in precious stones
Is there such beauty like that of Ma-ry
Hallelu-iah w'Ha-lleluiah, Jo`a-chim's daughter

On the Saints

The prophets and the - apostles are likened to
Shining stars- in the creation
They enlighten earth by their pure doc-trine
Hallelu-iah w'Ha-lleluiah, So Christ - called them light

O Martyrs, beg for - mercy on our sinful ge-neration
That God protect us
And overthrow Satan and his a-rmies
Hallelu-iah w'Ha-lleluiah, May your- pray'rs help us

On One Saint

On the day of your - remembrance, O St. Stephen
Our Father - the creatures rejoice
And sing praise to Christ, who magnified- you
Hallelu-iah w'Ha-lleluiah, may your - pray'rs help us

On Friday

On Friday, the Lord - of creation stretched His hands
On the Cross - and of His own will
Tasted death and not the fruit Adam- ate
Hallelu-iah w'Ha-lleluiah, He re-stored Adam

On Friday, the Church - beheld Christ on the height of
Golgotha - and bowed down to Him
And worshipped Him saying "Glory to- you!"
Hallelu-iah w'Ha-lleluiah, "who came- and saved me".

On Repentance

Day after day I - promise that tomorrow I
will repent -, yet my days have passed
and my sins remain, Lord, pour Your me-rcy
Hallelu-iah w'Ha-lleluiah, and grace- upon me

Lord, extend Your grace - let Your bounty flow over
The whole world. - Grant peace to leaders,
Unity to the churches and priests- and
Hallelu-iah w'Ha-lleluiah, forgive-ness to us

On the Departed

Our Lord and Savior, - may the dead who received Your
Flesh and Blood - hear Your voice calling:
"Come, enter, and inherit the Kingdom"
Hallelu-iah w'Ha-lleluiah, "and life - eternal"

I passed by a tomb - and contemplated the way
Of the world; - the slave and his lord
Are equal and kings who have depart-ed
Hallelu-iah w'Ha-lleluiah, have lost their pow`er

PETHGOMO

(Tone 1/ Ninne prathi vadhamettu nithyam njangal)

For Your sake we are slain every day - Halleluiah, Halleluiah
We are counted as sheep - for slaughter

Do not turn Your face from us - Halleluiah, Halleluiah
Do not forget our - affliction...*Barekmor*

+ Glory be to the Father, Son and Holy Spirit
Unto the ages of ages and forevermore.

EQBO

(O Sohde Qadishe/ Vimalanmar...)

O Holy - Martyrs! You -
Endured suff'ring and tor<u>ments</u> from imp`i`ous ju-dges
Behold - your reward is kept in the Lord's bridal cha-mber
May your pray'r be - for us a house - of - refuge
Stoumen Kalos Kurielaison

QOLO

(Sohdau Atun/ Ekathanujan than sahadere…)

O Holy Martyrs - You belov'd of the first born Son
You were slain for Him
And for His love you – Endured torments and were offered
As a sacrifice
Bless`ed is He – Who has magnified your mem`o`ry
O Holy Martyrs…*Barekmor*

+ Glory be to the Father, Son and Holy Spirit
Unto the ages of ages and forevermore.

Glory to You, Lord – for in all times there are just men
Who appease Your will:
In the first ages, - Noah, Abraham, Isaac, and Jacob
Moses, Elijah;
And in this age– the bless'd martyrs will pray with the blood
Which flowed from their necks

Lord have mercy upon us and help us!

BO'UTHO of MOR JACOB

Make us share Lord – in the mem'ry – of Your mother
And of Your saints – by their pray'rs have – mercy on us

How fair is the – day of mem'ry – of the bless`ed
Virgin Mary – who became the – Mother of God
By her pray'rs may – the Lord remove – the rod of wrath
From every place, – which honors her – feast day in faith

How fair is the – hope, which our Lord – gave to the dead
In She`ol when – He lay down like – them, beside them
O Death is slain! – rise and come forth – you dead ones from
Within the grave – sing praise to Him – who raised you up

Above in heav'n – and here in the – church on the earth
Make good mem'ry – of Your mother, - saints and the dead

Turn to ***Concluding Prayer of Vespers (p. 9)***

COMPLINE of DAY SIX [Friday]

Qaumo (p. 5)... Introductory Prayers (p.10)

QOLO

(Sohdau Atun/ Ninnodu paapam)

We know that our sins
Are great Lord and we know that – great are Your mercies
And if Your mercy
Should not persuade you, we shall – perish from our sins
Take not away
Lord Your hand from us, whom you have saved – by Your precious blood...*Barekmor*

+ Glory be to the Father, Son and Holy Spirit
Unto the ages of ages and forevermore.

If a slave offends
His master he takes refuge - in his master's friend
By that friend's pleading
The master forgives the slave – of his offences
We take refuge
In Your Cross that Your mercy may come – quickly upon us
Lord have mercy upon us and help us!

BO'UTHO of MOR JACOB

O Lord, - our Lord, we – call to You – come to our – aid
Hear our – requests and – have mercy – upon our – souls

Adam – instructed – his children – of what rea-son
He and – Eve were called – to depart – from Para-dise
He spoke – to them of – his former – author-ity
And of – his fall and – his exile – when he was – shamed:

It is – not fitting – for the foot – that ran to – the
Tree to – tread the ho-ly place when – it is not – clean
It is – not right for – the hand that – plucked the fruit – in
Eden – to wave o-ver the off-'ring of the Lord"

Christ, who– came and walked– on the earth- and uproot-ed
Its thorns, - by You A-dam returned – to Paradise

Kurielaison, Kurielaison, Kurielaison

Turn to ***Psalms of Compline (p. 10)***

NIGHT VIGIL of DAY SIX [Friday]

Qaumo (p.5)... Introductory Prayer (p.13)... Psalms of Night (p.13)

ENIYONO

(Etheer Qum Bnayn Nuhro/ Druthithan suthare...)

Awake and rise - O you sons of light
And give glory to the Lord
Who in His mercy - suffered to redeem us

By the pray'rs of - the virgin Mary
The Mother who brought You forth
Have mercy on the - Church redeemed by Your Cross

By the pray'rs and - by the petitions
Of the prophets, apostles
And the bless'd martyrs - strengthen the Holy Church

By the pray'rs of - the holy martyrs
Who suffered and died for You
Have mercy on the - Church redeemed by Your Cross

By the pray'rs and - by the peititions
Of the noble St. (Moses)
Have mercy on the - Church redeemed by Your Cross...*Barekmor*

+ Glory be to the Father, Son and Holy Spirit
Unto the ages of ages and forevermore.

Glory to You, - the Son, our Savior
To the Father who sent You
And exaltation - to the Holy Spirit

Kurieleison, Kurieleison, Kurieleison

Turn to the ***Introductory Prayer of 1st Qaumo (p. 14)***

There are two sets of prayer used for the 1st Qaumo of Lilio of Friday. The first is used from the Sancitification of the Church to the Great Lent (p.158); the second from the Great Lent to the Sanctification of the Church (p. 159).

1st QAUMO – *From Sanctification of the Church to Great Lent*

EQBO
(Faradaiso)

I will sing of the virgin, who by grace
Became the mother of the Lord of all
She conceived without man and without seed
And bore fruit without being joined in marriage
She was a marvel and bore a wonder
The learn`ed cannot search out this myst'ry

Lord have mercy; Lord have mercy, Lord have mercy
(Kurieleison, Kurieleison, Kurieleison)

Lord, have mercy upon us
Lord, be kind and have mercy
Answer, Lord, and have mercy

Glory be to You, O Lord
Glory be to You, O Lord
Glory be to You, our hope forever. *Barekmor*

QOLO
(l'Maryam Yoldath Aloho)

May mem'ry be made of the Mother of God
With the Prophets, Apostles, and the Martyrs
And the Children of the Church upon the earth
May good mem'ry be made now and forever…*Barekmor*

+ Glory be to the Father, Son and Holy Spirit
Unto the ages of ages and forevermore.

Glory to the Son of God Who willed to come
From the womb of the Bless`ed Virgin Mary
And saved the people from err`or, by His Birth,
Exalting her mem'ry; may her pray'rs help us

Lord have mercy upon us and help us!

BO'UTHO of MOR JACOB

O bless`ed one, may your pray'rs be with us always
May the Lord hear your pray'rs and have mercy on us

You bore, embraced, and cherished like a little child
The hero of the worlds who bears earth by gesture
Bless`ed are you, for from you came forth the Savior
Who in his zeal bound Satan who held us captive

Glory to the Most High, who departed the heights
And in humility dwelt in a humble girl
Good One, who exalts the mem'ry of your mother
Have pity on those who honor her festival

By the pray'r of her who carried you for nine months
O Son of God, remove from us the scourge of wrath

Turn to the ***Praise of the Cherubim (p. 14)***

OR

1st QAUMO – *From Great Lent to Qudosh Idto*

EQBO
(Faradaiso)

I looked and beheld three different crosses;
That on the right is alive and not dead
That on the left is dead and not alive
The one in the middle makes me marvel
It is like a man who wakes while he sleeps
And lives while he dies, like a Son of God

Lord have mercy; Lord have mercy, Lord have mercy
(Kurieleison, Kurieleison, Kurieleison)

Lord, have mercy upon us
Lord, be kind and have mercy
Answer, Lord, and have mercy

Glory be to You, O Lord
Glory be to You, O Lord
Glory be to You, our hope forever. *Barekmor*

QOLO

(Quqoyo)

From Rome, the city of kings, to Jerusalem
Helena the Queen arrived to adore the Cross
    She asked the Jews - "Where shall I find it?"
    They answered her - "Go seek the rabbi
If you take hold of him he will show you the place
Where the cross, which you have been seeking is buried;"
    Halleluiah - the cross of our Lord...*Barekmor*

+ Glory be to the Father, Son and Holy Spirit
Unto the ages of ages and forevermore.

Emman`u`el our God was hung upon the wood
And the Son of the Almighty inclined His head
    Upon the wood - His spirit left Him
    But His essence - stayed in His body
He left His human life, not His eternal one
For crucifying the Lord, the Jews will repent
    Halleluiah - O Lord have mercy!
Lord have mercy upon us and help us!

BO'UTHO of MOR JACOB

Son who by Your Cross delivered the Church from sin
Grant her Your peace and keep her children by the Cross

    The rabbi stood and girded himself at the site
    And dug and found three crosses which lay together;
    The mother of the king was sad because of this
    For she did not know which was the cross of her Lord

The rabbi, Judas, said to her, "Do not be grieved
For the Lord lives who will show you which is His cross"
The Father was pleased to show you the Cross of light
By means of a dead young man who was brought along

    When they placed them one after the other on him
    The people cried, "Living Cross, show us your pow`er"
    The dead young man saw the Cross of light and rose up
    All who saw gave glory to Him who raised him up

By the mercy you showed to the thief on the right
Son of God, have compassion and mercy on us

Turn to the ***Praise of the Cherubim (p. 14)***

2nd QAUMO

Turn to ***Introductory Prayer of 2nd Qaumo (p. 15)***

EQBO

(Faradaiso)

In mem'ry of the saints, let us gather
And offer praise to the Lord of the saints
That He may make His peace dwell in the world
    And that He may gather us with the saints
So that when His majesty is revealed
With them, we may praise Him without ceasing

Lord have mercy; Lord have mercy, Lord have mercy
(Kurieleison, Kurieleison, Kurieleison)

Lord, have mercy upon us
Lord, be kind and have mercy
Answer, Lord, and have mercy
Glory be to You, O Lord
Glory be to You, O Lord
Glory be to You, our hope forever. *Barekmor*

QOLO

(l'Maryam Yoldath Aloho)

A perfume rose from the bones of the martyrs
And gave joy in the heights to the King of kings
The watchers in heaven rejoiced at their strength
And the Church celebrates the day of their feasts... *Barekmor*

+ Glory be to the Father, Son and Holy Spirit
Unto the ages of ages and forevermore.

O Martyrs, friends of the Son, what made you drunk
So that you were crowned with the sword, not cast down?
"We saw the blood of Christ and it made us drunk
And we did not feel torment for love of Him"
Lord have mercy upon us and help us!

BO'UTHO of MOR EPHREM

Lord have mercy upon us
By the pray'rs of Your servants
By their pray'rs and petitions
Have mercy upon our souls

Martyrs, you are like eagles
And are more swift than the wind
You answer calls on the sea
And answer, too, on dry land

The martyrs sang to the Son
In the midst of their suff'ring
And behold, the Church sings praise
Upon the day of their feast

Lord have mercy upon us
By the pray'rs of Your servants
By their pray'rs and petitions
Have mercy upon our souls

Turn to the ***Praise of the Cherubim (p. 15)***

3rd QAUMO

Turn to ***Introductory Prayer of 3rd Qaumo (p. 15)***

EQBO

(Faradaiso)

Paradise is the dwelling of the saints
Paradise is the dwelling of the just,
Paradize is the dwelling of the chaste
Paradise is the life which has no end –
The marriage-feast which does not pass away
Bless`ed are they who find inheritance there

Lord have mercy; Lord have mercy, Lord have mercy
(Kurieleison, Kurieleison, Kurieleison)

Lord, have mercy upon us
Lord, be kind and have mercy
Answer, Lord, and have mercy

Glory be to You, O Lord
Glory be to You, O Lord
Glory be to You, our hope forever. *Barekmor*

QOLO

(l'Maryam Yoldath Aloho)

Help us, O God and Savior, halleluiah
"Rise, help us and deliver us," said Adam
"For Eve and the serpent have come upon me
And I am overcome because of this fruit
I have lost the glory in which I was clothed"…*Barekmor*

+ Glory be to the Father, Son and Holy Spirit
Unto the ages of ages and forevermore.

The evil one has bound me with chains of sin
And I have been tied to sin for a long time
May Your compassion, O Lord, cut from my limbs
The bonds and the fetters of iniquity

Lord have mercy upon us and help us

BO'UTHO of MOR BALAI

Renew Your creatures by the res'rrection,
Your worshippers who have slept in Your hope.

Give rest and pardon to the dead, O Lord,
Who sleep in hope and await Your coming.

Lord, with Abraham, Isaac and Jacob,
Make Your servants rest, those who sleep in hope.

Their bodies and souls shall cry together:
"Bless'd is He who will come and raise the dead."

Turn to ***p. 16 to continue Night Vigil***

QOLO of the DAY
(l'Maryam Yoldath Aloho)

Behold the time of pray'er, O (St. Ivanios)
Stand and intercede at the head of your flock
Stretch forth your hand like Moses and bless all those
Who hasten to the sound of your gentle voice...*Barekmor*

+ Glory be to the Father, Son and Holy Spirit
Unto the ages of ages and forevermore.

Praise to the Father who chose you, St. (Andrew)
And to the Son who honors your mem`o`ry;
Worshipped is the Holy Spirit who crowns you
By your pray'rs, may mercy be on us always
Lord have mercy upon us and help us

BO'UTHO of MOR JACOB

Make us share Lord in the mem'ry of Your mother
And of Your saints; by their pray'rs have mercy on us

The martyrs' death confounded the crucifiers
For by their death, the Cross showed its pow`er from God
When people laid down their lives because of the cross
Earth saw the pow'r of Him who had been crucified

When the King mounted the Cross, salvation appeared
And awakened the captives who were drowned in sleep
He called out to the dead, "Proceed forth from the grave
See my salvation, for I died that you might live"

There in heaven and in the Church here on the earth
Remember Your mother and saints and all the dead

Turn to the ***Hymn of the Angels (p. 20)***

MATINS of DAY SIX [Friday]

Qaumo (p. 5)... Introductory Prayer (p.21)... Psalms of Matins (p.21)

ENIYONO

(Sleebo Otho d'Shaino/ Shubha chinam thaan sleeba)

The Cross is the sign of peace
And the sign of vict`o`ry
By the Cross we have been saved;
And in it we all glory

In the camp of Isra`e`l
The bronze serpent was set up
As a sign and surety
Of the Cross, which brings forth life

Bless'd is He who made the Cross
A ladder for Adam's sons
By which prophets, apostles,
And the martyrs ascended

The Cross conquered and conquers
The Cross has conquered Satan
May the Cross be a stronghold
To all who confess the Cross

We fear not the evil one
Because the Lord is with us
We are clothed in His armor
And in it we all glory

May He who carried the Cross
On His shoulder from Zi`on,
Sprinkle His dew of mercy
Upon the bones of the dead

O Lord, may the departed
Who confessed the Trinity
Be received in Your Kingdom
As You promised to the thief...*Barekmor*

+ Glory be to the Father, Son and Holy Spirit
Unto the ages of ages and forevermore.

Glory to Jesus, who was
Crucified on Golgotha
He cried out and rocks were rent
The dead arose and sang praise...*Amin*

*Turn to **Psalm 113 (p. 23)***

EQBO

(Fsaqth Basleebokh/ Adhipathiyude akhilesha)

By Your Cross You cut off the head of the ev-il tyrant
By Your valor you loosed the hold of greedy - Death on us
So we cry to You
Glory to the Pow'r of Your be`ing Lord - of - all
Stoumen Kalos, Kurieleison

QOLO

(Bgaw Mashkan Sabno/ Sthothrathin baliyarpipin...)

Offer Him sacrifices of praise
Moses called on God
With incense in the earthly tabernacle and God heard
And answered his pray'r
Grant, O Lord, that in Your Church the incense of your servants
Halleluiah
May be acceptable like that of Aaron, the high priest...*Barekmor*

+ Glory be to the Father, Son and Holy Spirit
Unto the ages of ages and forevermore.

Praise to the Strong One
Who left the ranks of the angels and descended and dwelt
In the virgin's womb
He entered her as God and came forth from her as God-man
Halleluiah
Come, you peoples, and praise God who became man to save us

On the Theotokos

Prophet Isaiah,
Declare to us of Him who is conceived of the virgin?
"He is the true God
Whose name is Emman`u`el and shall be called a wonder
Halleluiah
Bless`ed is the Lord of the prophets who fulfilled their words

O Holy Virgin
Upon whom the pow`er of the Most High God descended
You bore the Savior;
On the day of your remembrance pray and beseech your Son
Halleluiah
That He may show mercy and compassion to the whole world

On the Cross

On top of the Cross
The Jews made a wine press and they pressed the grape of blessing
But did not taste it
Instead the Holy Church received it and takes joy in it
Halleluiah
Her children drink of it and rejoice in it forever

On the Saints

Holy Apostles,
Preachers of the faith who went forth like ploughmen through the earth
Pray on our behalf
That tares be uprooted from us and the good seed not choke
Halleluiah
Bless`ed is He who sowed His gospel throughout all the earth

I saw the martyrs
How their blood is poured out on the earth and their heart is full
Of exultation
And they say: "How sweet it is to die for God who gives life
Halleluiah
O Savior of the world, make us inherit the kingdom

On One Saint

Father, St. (Thomas)
Visit your flock now for the wolves have torn it to pieces
And it is scattered
And there is no shepherd to gather it back together
Halleluiah
O Christ, the Good Shepherd, gather Your flock which is scattered

On Repentance

"How bless`ed am I,"
Cried the thief on the Cross at the right hand of the Most High
"How bless`ed am I"
Make me worthy to open the door closed by Adam's sin
Halleluiah
That I may enter with face unveiled and cry, 'Praise to You'

O Vast Treas`u`ry
O Rich One who never grows poor and High Wall of Refuge
Strengthen our weakness
Wash away the stain in our souls; grant us strength to praise You;
Halleluiah
And give thanks to You for Your grace, O Savior of the world

On the Departed

May our departed
Who had lived long in the world of suff'ring and left this earth
Dwell with the righteous
In Eden, a place of joy, which is raised above all fear
Halleluiah
Christ, have compassion on them on the day of Your coming

When the Lord appears
To judge the living and the dead whom He fashioned from dust
May all our brethren
Who have departed this world be placed at Your right hand side
Halleluiah
O Christ our hope, may they take their pleasure in Your Kingdom
Lord have mercy upon us and help us!

QOLO

(Dehato lo Nehte/ Pulariyil en naadham kelkaname – Haleluiah)

Lord in the morning You shall hear my voice, Halleluiah
In the morning when Your light shall appear
Creation shall come to adore Your Cross
A message shall come to the Holy Church:
'The pow'r of the Cross has conquered Satan' – Halleluiah
Ev'ry man shall give praise and thanksgiving…*Barekmor*

+ Glory be to the Father, Son and Holy Spirit
Unto the ages of ages and forevermore.

Praise, thanksgiving and honor to the Son;
Remembrance to the virgin who bore Him
She was preserved intact and nourished Him
She brought forth for us the first-born of God – Halleluiah
In truth He is the Savior of the world

On the Theotokos

Mary had been orphaned of her parents
As Moses commanded, priests brought her up
When her father and her mother had died
The Lord of the prophets came and bless'd her – Halleluiah
May her pray'r be a stronghold for our souls

The mighty Lord God of strength is with us
Whom Mary bore in her virginity
As Isaiah, son of Amos, foretold:
"Behold a virgin shall conceive and bear – Halleluiah
A wonder who shall be called 'God with us'"

On the Cross

The Holy Cross has sanctified our souls
The Cross has pardoned all our offenses
The Cross has cast down Satan and his pow'r
And has given vict'ry to the faithful – Halleluiah
Keep us, Lord, beneath the wings of Your Cross

On the Saints

The Church built upon the faith of Simon
Which was set on seventy-two pillars
Is high`er than the mountain of Cardu (Gen 8:4)
The Architect who built it dwells on high – Halleluiah
Bless'd is He who set His altar in it

The servants of the Most High God entered
They stood in the place of judgment and said:
"We have loved You, Lord, and hated the world
Grant us vict'ry over the evil one – Halleluiah
That heathens will not ask, 'Where is your God?'

On Friday

On Friday, the sixth day, the wicked men
Set up the Cross of the Almighty God
On Friday, they pierced His side with a lance
From where the blood and water of life flowed – Halleluiah
For those who confess and believe in Him

Tell me, Friday, why do all the churches
In all places give you such great honor?
"Adam, head of mankind, was formed on me
And upon me he entered Paradise – Halleluiah
And on me the Savior was crucified

On the Morning

How fearful is the morning when the Lord
Will come and the creation will tremble,
The judge will sit; the books will be opened
He will bring to light all the hidden things – Halleluiah
You who know all things have mercy on me

On Repentance

Your judgment is harsh and our sins are great
Justice threatens and I cannot escape
When You come, Lord, to the place of judgment
Do not enter into judgment with us – Halleluiah
Do not remember our faults, O Just Judge

One of the wise men in his book taught me:
"Keep away from one who is deceitful
His lips *smile* at you, his heart is cunning
He lays snares for you while be`ing your friend – Halleluiah
Rescue us, Lord, from the deceitful friend

On the Departed

Christ, our Savior, who came down from heaven
And hung on the Cross and brought salvation,
Who overcame and conquered the devil.
Give joy and good rest, Lord, to Your servants – Halleluiah
Who were counted among Your faithful flock

Lord, the faithful dead await Your coming
That You may fulfill Your promise to them:
"He who eats my Body and drinks my Blood
Abides in me and I shall be in him" - Halleluiah
In Your mercy, Lord, raise up Your servants

QUQLION

(Tone 6/ Velum shathrukale ninaal njangal)

Through You we shall strike down our enemies - Halleluiah
In Your name we shall trample on our foes

You have saved us from our foes - Halleluiah
And put to shame all our enemies…*Barekmor*

+ Glory be to the Father, Son and Holy Spirit
Unto the ages of ages and forevermore.

EQBO

(At Basleebokh/ Maanavavargatheporil)

O Lord by Your Cross You have
Overthrown the enemy
Who had prevailed over us
And therefore we all come to
Exalt Your life-gi-ving Cross…*Stoumen Kalos, Kurieleison*

QOLO

(Lokh Moriyo Qorenan/ Cherkuka chirakin keezhil njangale naadha-Hal..)

Beneath your wings protect us Lord, Halleluiah
In the morning the living Cross will appear
Throughout the earth it will manifest - vict`o`ry
All those who had denied it will confess it
Bless'd martyrs will rejoice in it and - receive crowns
By it we - confess and worship
We have life - by Your saving work
Bless'd is He who made His Cross, for us, - a stronghold. *Barekmor*

+ Glory be to the Father, Son and Holy Spirit
Unto the ages of ages and forevermore.

King Constantine looked in the sky and he saw
A great token of wonder, the sign – of the Cross
When he looked into the vision, he was told:
'By this sign of life you shall gain the – vict`o`ry'
He cast down – the images and
Gave honor – to the Cross alone
Bless'd is He who made His Cross, for us, – a stronghold
Lord have mercy upon us and help us!

BO'UTHO of MOR JACOB

Son who – by Your Cross delivered – the Church from sin
Grant her – Your peace and keep her chil-dren by Your Cross

The wood – of the Cross went up from – Jerusalem
And was – honored in all places – through which it passed
The King – Constantine heard that the – Cross had arrived
He took – his army with him and – went to meet it

His mo-ther, Queen Helen, wrote a – letter to him:
"Behold, - the Cross has arrived. Rise – and receive it
He took – with him the high priests and – the reverend priests
That he – might honor and adore - it with reverence

By the – mercy You showed to the – thief on the right
Son of – God, have compassion and – mercy on us

Turn to ***Concluding Prayer of Matins (p. 23)***

THIRD HOUR of DAY SIX [Friday]

Qaumo (p. 5)... Introductory Prayer (p. 24)

QOLO

(Sohdau Atun/ Moonammaniyilumennerathum)

At the Third *Hour* and at all times, we will adore
The life-giving Cross,
And we sign ourselves with it for it is our hope
And strong protection
By night and day – from the evil one and his pow`ers –
It delivers us. *Barekmor*

+ Glory be to the Father, Son and Holy Spirit
Unto the ages of ages and forevermore.

At the Third *Hour*, Adam ate the fruit of death from
The tree in Eden
At the Sixth Ho`ur, the Lord ascended the Cross
For His servant's sake
At the Ninth *Hour* – Christ, from the Cross restored Adam to
His inheritance.

Lord have mercy upon us and help us!

BO'UTHO of MOR JACOB

Son who by Your Cross delivered the Church from sin
Grant her Your peace and keep her children by Your Cross

Son of God in whose Cross the creation rejoiced,
Let my mind rejoice in the precious Cross of light;
As You have made me worthy to speak of the Cross,
Make Your Church worthy of the marriage feast of life.

Great Saviour, who saved your Church from e`rror and death,
Save me in my weakness on the day of judgment;
On this festival, we assemble at Your Cross;
On that day, may I see Your mercy and praise You.

By the mercy You showed to the thief on the right
Son of God, have compassion and mercy on us

Qaumo (p. 5)

SIXTH HOUR of DAY SIX [Friday]

Qaumo (p. 5)…Introductory Prayer (p. 25)

QOLO

(Sohdau Atun/ Baalyathil thaanettudayon nin…)

Bless'd are you Mary, whom our God chose from childhood
And magnified you
The bread of off'rings nourished you at His table
In the house of God
Priests honored you – and the angel greeted you with peace
And God dwelt in you…*Barekmor*

+ Glory be to the Father, Son and Holy Spirit

Martyrs upon martyrs came before judges and
Did not deny Christ
So they were slain by the sword and their blood flowed out
On those who killed them
The Lord saw them–and their endurance and he crowned them
May their pray'rs help us.

Unto the ages of ages and forevermore.

Our Lord gave us a good hope and encouragement –
Regarding the dead
He said the *hour* will come when they shall hear His voice
And will be raised up
The evil ones – will be sent to judgment and the just –
Will receive new life

Lord have mercy upon us and help us!

*Turn to **Bo'utho of Mor Balai (p. 25)***

NINTH HOUR of DAY SIX [Friday]

Qaumo (p. 5)... Introductory Prayer (p. 27)

QOLO

(d'Trayhun Olme/ Naadha thavakamirulokam)

Your authority, O Lord
Is present in both the worlds
Keep the living by Your Cross
And absolve the faithful dead... *Barekmor*

+ Glory be to the Father, Son and Holy Spirit
Unto the ages of ages and forevermore.

Glory to You, Who gives life
To those who lie in the tombs
Glory be to Your Father
And to the Holy Spirit

Lord have mercy upon us and help us!

BO'UTHO of MOR BALAI

Renew Your creatures by the res'rrection,
Your worshippers who have slept in Your hope.
    Give rest and pardon to the dead, O Lord,
    Who sleep in hope and await Your coming.
Lord, with Abraham, Isaac and Jacob,
Make Your servants rest, those who sleep in hope.
    Their bodies and souls shall cry together:
    "Bless'd is He who will come and raise the dead

Qaumo (p.5)

VESPERS OF DAY SEVEN [Saturday]

Qaumo (p. 5)...Introductory Prayer (p. 8)...Psalms of Vespers (p. 8)

EQBO

(Yaumono/ Mruthiyarnore…)

O departed, - bless'd are you
On that day of re-surrection
The Living Body, which you ate
And the Absolving Blood you drank
Shall raise you up at – His right hand…*Staumen Kalos Kurielaison*

QOLO

(Vaazhthuka naadhane enmaname…)

Bless the Lord, O my soul
Grant rest, O Messiah King
To the souls of Your servants in peace
With all of Your saints
Where death nor suff`ering reign
Nor where sorrow rules but instead life
Which is eternal…*Barekmor*

+ Glory be to the Father, Son and Holy Spirit
Unto the ages of ages and forevermore.

You've done wonders for the dead
So I called upon You all day and
Stretched my hands toward You
The mighty shall praise You and
Tell of Your grace and that You are He
Who raises the dead

On the Theotokos

The Most High came forth from you
And humbled Himself in order to
Raise fallen Adam
He honored and magnified
Your mem`o`ry here and in heaven;
May your pray'rs help us

Prophet Moses saw a fire
Which rested on a bush and it was
Not burned by the flames
Like that bush the virgin was
Not burned by the flame of the Son of
God who dwelt in her

On the Saints

Peace be with all the prophets
And peace be with all the apostles
And with the martyrs,
For they loved the Lord of peace
Peace be with the holy Church in whom
Dwell the sons of peace

Like the wall of a city
Moses placed the bones of Joseph in
The Isr'aelite camp
Likewise, Your bones, O Martyrs
Are a stronghold for our souls which guards
Us beneath its wings

On Repentance

When Joseph was dying he
Said to his brothers, "Do not leave me
In a foreign land
Bring up my bones from Egypt
That I may go with you and the Lord
Will be your helper"

"Be not sad, brother Joseph,
Let your mind not be afraid that we
May go and leave you
We remember the kindness
You showed us in Egypt when you did
Not recall our faults

On the Departed

Adam stretched his hand and ate
The fruit from the tree of knowledge in
Which death was hidden
Our Lord ascended the Cross
And tasted death for him and restored
His inheritance

The just do not taste the death
Which is fore'er, but their bodies rest
As it were in sleep
Until resurrection day
Their bodies remain in the earth and
Shall rise and give praise
Lord have mercy upon us and help us!

QOLO

(Deivam nammodu krupacheyum…)

May God have mercy on us
In the evening when the just
Complete their labor for You
Complete Your work in our souls
And protect us from Satan… *Barekmor*

+ Glory be to the Father, Son and Holy Spirit
Unto the ages of ages and forevermore.

In the service of evening,
Have compassion on us and
When You sit at judgment day
Raise us up at Your right hand

On the Theotokos

O pride of the faithful ones,
Offer pray'rs on our behalf
To the Only Begotten
That He have mercy on us

O virgin, who was the source
From whom life was transmitted
Beseech and implore Your Son
That He have mercy on us

On the Saints

May prophets and apostles,
Who preached You by the Spirit,
And martyrs who died for You
Intercede with You for us

Pray with us, O holy saints,
To Him whose will you fulfilled
That He may keep from us all
Punishments and rods of wrath

On One Saint

Your mem'ry, O St. (Stephen)
Is kept here and in heaven
May your pray'r be a help to
those who honor your mem'ry

On Repentance

At the door of Your mercy
Knocks the voice of our pray`er
Keep not from Your worshippers
The answer to their requests

O Good One, We call on You,
To help us in our weakness
Lord, hear the voice of our pray'r
Answer us in Your mercy

On the Departed

Lord, may all the departed
Who clothed You in baptism
Be clothed by Your right hand in
glor'ious garb in Your Kingdom

May the names of all the dead
Whose mem'ry we celebrate
Be written in Your Kingom
In the Book of Life, O Lord

PETHGOMO

(Makkalilappan…)

As a father shows mercy to his children - Halleluiah, Halle-luiah
So the Lord shows mercy to those - who fear him

For He knows how we are formed - Halleluiah, Halle-luiah
He remembers that - we are dust

As for man his days are like grass, Halleluiah, Halle-luiah
Like the flow`er of the field - so he blooms

When the wind blows over it, it is no more–Halleluiah, Halle-luiah
And its place remembers - it no more…*Barekmor*

+ Glory be to the Father, Son and Holy Spirit
Unto the ages of ages and forevermore.

EQBO

(Punaruthaanathin…)

The thunder of the
Resurrection will thunder over - the depths of She`ol
Death will hear and be dismayed, O Lord
Renew Your servants - who slept in - Your hope
Stoumen Kalos Kurielaison

QOLO

(Trayhun Olme / Arppichabraham dhoopam…)

Abraham offered incense
Noah offered sacrifice
We offer - incense for - Your servants
Lord, give rest - to them…*Barekmor*

+ Glory be to the Father, Son and Holy Spirit
Unto the ages of ages and forevermore.

Have mercy - on our dead
Who like seed - are laid in the earth
As you will - O Lord, raise - them up and
Comfort those - who mourn

Lord have mercy upon us and help us

BO'UTHO of MOR JACOB

O Lord, give rest to Your servants - among the just
In that kingdom, - which has no end among the saints

All who enter this evil world - are worn out by
It and those who - love it are not allowed to stay
Like citizens and heirs they la-bor in the world
But like nomads - and pilgrims, they depart from it

In the days of their life men command, as if God
But at the time of their end they all die like beasts
Yesterday they were proud kings exalted with pow'r
Today they are dead, fallen, cast down and wretch`ed

Christ, who prayed that the cup of death might pass from You
Make to pass from us the cup of the second death

Turn to ***Concluding Prayer of Vespers (p. 9)***

COMPLINE of DAY SEVEN [Saturday]

Qaumo (p. 5)... Introductory Prayers (p.10)

QOLO

(d'Habloh l'Eedtokh/ Sheelippikenne…)

Teach me the way of - Your commandments, O Lord
And I will keep them
I will live - in grace
Lord, guard the doors of - my limbs that lie open
Lest the treasure of
Your gifts be -stolen...*Barekmor*

+ Glory be to the Father, Son and Holy Spirit
Unto the ages of ages and forevermore.

Behold, at that time - on the day of judgment
When our en`e`my,
Satan, is vanquished
Let us, my brethren - be diligent and watch
With fasting and pray'r
For eter-nal life

Lord have mercy upon us and help us

BO'UTHO of MOR JACOB

O Lord,- our Lord, we - call to You - come to our - aid
Hear our - requests and - have mercy - upon our - souls

Woe to - the earth when - the last day- shall come and- when
It shall - be corrupt-ted by sin - and defile-ment
The earth - will cry out - like a mo-ther who gives - birth
And when - wars and di-sasters rise - she will co-llapse

The world - will cease from - sacrifice - and service -; instead
Greed - and love of - money shall - prevail on - earth
In the - last days na-tion shall rise - against na-tion
And the -towns and ci-ties shall be - devasta-ted

Lord, care -for the chur-ches and mon-asteries - for
The day- is near when- Your praise shall- cease within-them

Kurielaison, Kurielaison, Kurielasion

Turn to ***Psalms of Compline (p. 10)***

NIGHT VIGIL of DAY SEVEN [Saturday]

Qaumo (p.5)... Introductory Prayer (p.13)... Psalms of Night (p.13)

ENIYONO

(L'iqoro Walteshbuhto/ Aathmavodu ninnardhrathaye)

To the honor and glory
Of Your lo-ving mercy
We rose up to sing to You
Lord of all, to You the praise

Angels on high cry to You:
"Holy, ho-ly, holy"
Men upon the earth hasten
To worship Your majesty

In Your mercy, O Lord God
Magnify – the mem'ry
Of your mother who bore You
And help us by her pray`ers

In Your mercy, O Lord God
Magnify – the mem'ry
Of prophets, apostles, and
Martyrs and help us through them

In Your mercy, O Lord God
Magnify – the mem'ry
Of the martyrs who were slain
And help us by their pray`ers

In Your mercy, O Lord God
Magnify – the mem'ry
Of the fathers and doctors
And help us by their pray`ers

In Your mercy, O Lord God
Magnify – the mem'ry
Of noble St. (Ignatius)
And help us by his pray`ers...*Barekmor*

+ Glory be to the Father, Son and Holy Spirit
Unto the ages of ages and forevermore.

We offer up a new praise
To Your lo-ving mercy
And sing songs of thanksgiving
To Your worshipful name, Lord
Kurieleison, Kurieleison, Kurieleison

Turn to the ***Introductory Prayer of 1st Qaumo (p. 14)***

1st QAUMO

EQBO

(Abo k'thab wo)

There were not two beings brought forth – from the Father and Mary
There was only one – brought forth from them both,
In spirit from the Father – and in flesh from the virgin
Lord have mercy; Lord have mercy, Lord have mercy
(Kurieleison, Kurieleison, Kurieleison)

Lord, have mercy upon us
Lord, be kind and have mercy
Answer, Lord, and have mercy

Glory be to You, O Lord
Glory be to You, O Lord
Glory be to You, our hope forever. *Barekmor*

QOLO

(Morahimin)

Like the smoke of sweet incense
May the mem'ry – of Mary please You
Who bore – You in purity
While in – her virginity
O Lord, make mem'ry of her
Here in the church – and above in heav'n... *Barekmor*

+ Glory be to the Father, Son and Holy Spirit
Unto the ages of ages and forevermore.

Glory be to the Father
Who did choose you – from the beginning
To His – Son be thanksgiving
Who did – take His flesh from you
Praise to the Holy Spirit
Who came down and – made you His temple
Lord have mercy upon us and help us

BO'UTHO of MOR JACOB

O bless`ed one, may your pray'rs be with us always
May the Lord hear your pray'rs and have mercy on us

Come, you who have discernment, and with love and faith
Let us honor the festival of the virgin
With watching and unceasing standing at pray`er
A double reward awaits those who honor her

May He who strengthened you, strengthen our assembly
May He call us to the marriage-chamber of light
May the Lord remember the living and the dead
Who have honored your festival and seek your pray'rs

By the pray'r of her who carried You for nine months
O Son of God, remove from us the scourge of wrath

Turn to the ***Praise of the Cherubim (p. 14)***

2nd QAUMO

Turn to the ***Introductory Prayer of 2nd Qaumo (p. 15)***

EQBO

(Abo k'thab wo)

Bless`ed are you holy ones, - bless'd in the gospel of Christ
Your names are written - in the book of life
Bless'd is He who honors you - and celebrates your feast-day

Lord have mercy; Lord have mercy, Lord have mercy
(Kurieleison, Kurieleison, Kurieleison)

Lord, have mercy upon us
Lord, be kind and have mercy
Answer, Lord, and have mercy
Glory be to You, O Lord
Glory be to You, O Lord
Glory be to You, our hope forever. *Barekmor*

QOLO

(Morahimin)

How fair is your remembrance
And how pleasant – the day of your feasts
You who – made the cross a bridge
And came – to the land of life
The Spirit rejoiced in you
And wove and placed – crowns upon your heads... *Barekmor*

+ Glory be to the Father, Son and Holy Spirit
Unto the ages of ages and forevermore.

You are truly physicians,
Bless`ed martyrs – to him who believes
Bless'd is – he who honors you
And who – takes part in your feasts
He shall be welcomed with you
And with you he – shall inherit life
Lord have mercy upon us and help us!

BO'UTHO of MOR EPHREM

Lord, have mercy upon us
By the pray'rs of Your servants
By their pray'rs and petitions
Have mercy upon our souls

May prophets who spoke of You,
The apostles who preached You,
And martyrs who died for You
Intercede with You for us

Pray for us, O holy ones
To the One whose will you did
That He may withdraw from us
The scourge and the rod of wrath

Lord, have mercy upon us
By the pray'rs of Your servants
By their pray'rs and petitions
Have mercy upon our souls

Turn to the ***Praise of the Cherubim (p. 15)***

3rd QAUMO

*Turn to **Introductory Prayer of 3rd Qaumo (p. 15)***

EQBO
(Abo k'thab wo)

Sleep charmed me and I slumbered – by the trees in Paradise
And then a wind breathed – and the trees were stirred
A sweet voice fell on my ears – I knew my sins were pardoned

Lord have mercy; Lord have mercy, Lord have mercy
(Kurieleison, Kurieleison, Kurieleison)

Lord, have mercy upon us
Lord, be kind and have mercy
Answer, Lord, have mercy

Glory be to You, O Lord
Glory be to You, O Lord
Glory be to You, our hope forever. *Barekmor*

QOLO
(Mshiho lo Tahme)

Remember us and do not forget us
Do not disregard us, Christ
Do not turn away from us
For we took refuge in You
Lead us in the way of life
And make us worthy, O Lord
To praise You by night and day…*Barekmor*

+ Glory be to the Father, Son and Holy Spirit
Unto the ages of ages and forevermore.

When the horn sounds in the heights
With the voice of the trumpet
The graves and rocks shall be rent
All the departed shall rise
Lord, have compassion on us
Raise us up at Your right hand

Lord have mercy upon us and help us

BO'UTHO of MOR BALAI

Renew Your creatures by the res'rrection,
Your worshippers who have slept in Your hope.

Give rest and pardon to the dead, O Lord,
Who sleep in hope and await Your coming.

Lord, with Abraham, Isaac and Jacob,
Make Your servants rest, those who sleep in hope.

Their bodies and souls shall cry together:
"Bless'd is He who will come and raise the dead."

Turn to ***p. 16 for continuation of Night Vigil***

QOLO of the DAY
(Morahimin/ Marthoma than praarthanayaal)

By the pray'r of St. (Michael)
May the Lord God - remove wrath from earth
And make - His peace and his calm
Dwell in - the Church throughout earth
And may those who honor Him
Be kept from harm - now and forever...*Barekmor*

+ Glory be to the Father, Son and Holy Spirit
Unto the ages of ages and forevermore.

"Neither fi`re nor the sword
Can remove me - from the love of Christ"
This is - what the Martyr George
Said be-fore the foes of Christ
"For the love of Him in me
I will refuse - all this world's pleasures"

Lord have mercy upon us and help us!

BO'UTHO of MOR EPHREM

Lord, have mercy upon us
By the pray`r of Your mother
By the pray`er of Your saints
Have mercy upon us all

The Son, brought forth divinely
In Spirit from the Father
And in flesh from the virgin,
Exalts Mary forever

You martyrs, who like heroes
Endured pain and received crowns
Beseech our God with loud cries
That He may show us mercy

Call and they shall rise swiftly,
Those who took Your flesh and blood
When You come to pass judgment
Take them to Your marriage-feast

Glory be to the Father
And Worship be to the Son;
Thanksgiving to the Spirit
And on us, mercy always

Lord have mercy upon us
By the pray'r of Your mother
By the pray`er of Your saints
Have mercy upon us all

*Turn to the **Hymn of the Angels (p. 20)***

MATINS of DAY SEVEN [Saturday]

Qaumo (p. 5)...Introductory Prayer (p.21)...Psalms of Matins (p.21)

ENIYONO

(Ninmey rakthangal...)

Judge not Your servants – *to whom You have* given
Your body and blood – as a pledge, O Lord

May Mary's mem'ry – be for our blessing
May her pray'r be a – refuge for our souls

Prophets, apostles – and holy martyrs
Entreat and beg for – mercy for us all

Let us beg the martyrs – let us beseech them
That for us they may – be intercessors

Lord, have mercy on us – O Judge who is just
Forgive our debts in – Your abounding grace

O Judge, who is just – *do not make us* enter
Into judgment and – *blot out our* offenses

Lord, give rest and pardon – to our departed
Who rest in Your hope – and await Your coming...*Barekmor*

+ Glory be to the Father, Son and Holy Spirit
Unto the ages of ages and forevermore.

Glory to Him who – magnifies the mem'ry
Of Mary and the Saints – and raises the dead...*Amin*

*Turn to **Psalm 113** (p. 23)*

EQBO

(Dhaarmikar sahaderum...)

Make us worthy of that morning – when the just rejoice
And the martyrs receive – reward for their labor.
Stoumen Kalos, Kurieleison

QOLO

(Aascharyam mrutharilaho nee katunnu...)

Behold, you who do wonders for the departed, Halleluiah
The Church – of the faithful makes – mem'ry of –departed
By the smoke of incense which – priests offer
May peace – of the Father reign – and Satan be cast down
And the Church will praise You, O – Life-Giver...*Barekmor*

+ Glory be to the Father, Son and Holy Spirit
Unto the ages of ages and forevermore.

Glory – to You, Lord at whose – voice arose Lazarus
After he had undergone – corruption
At Your – entrance the daughter – of Jairus awakened
At the sound of Your voice the – dead will rise

On the Theotokos

Without – pen and without ink – Gabr`i`el – brought a le-tter
full of peace and came to- Mary and said:
"Peace – be with you the Lord – is with you – and the Sa-vior
Of Creation shall come – forth from you

The rock – in the desert, which – brought forth flow-ing water
Was clearly a figure of – you, Virgin
From whom, - into creation, – came forth the – Son of God
Who is the True Rock as Paul – has written

On the Saints

"On the – Rock of Faith proclaimed – by Simon I am built – and I am
Not afraid" the – Church answered
And said – "The waves beat against me but they – shake me not; -
Nestorius opposed me and – met his fall

Martyrs, – for what reason did – you despise this world, which
Is temp`o`rary, but which – all men love
Because – it is deceitful – in its pleasures, and it
Has hated those who love it – throughout time

On Repentance

All the – earth has not sinned a-gainst You as I have sinned
The proud have not angered You – as I have
My life – is short, death approaches – and what shall I do?
By the love, which sent You a-bsolve my debts

Behold – repentance calls you – O sinner, rise and go
With her in joy and take re-fuge beneath
Her wings – Do not promise day – by day: "I will repent"
Lest today or tomorrow – death should come

On the Departed

The wise – Creator in His – divine wisdom has bound
The whole world beneath the yoke – of death and
Removes – exalted kings from – their high places and He
Removes the mighty judges – from their seats

Our Lord – came to Bethany – to visit – La`za`rus
And He found him laid four days – in the tomb
He called – to him with His voice – and raised him up and said:
"I am the Son of God who – makes to die – and live"
Lord have mercy upon us and help us!

QOLO

(B'safro Tobayn/ Naadhan ishtam niravetum shushrushakasangam)

The servants who did the will of God
At morning the lab`o`rers
Who have worked in the Lord's vineyard
Will ask Him for their wages:
"We have worked morning till eve".
And the Lord will answer them:
"I will give you – my promise – and I will add more:
An unveiled face at my throne"…*Barekmor*

+ Glory be to the Father, Son and Holy Spirit
Unto the ages of ages and forevermore.

Glory to the first-born Son
Who went to She`ol and slew death
Adam saw and was relieved
And bowed his head and worshipped
And he said before his Lord:
"Forgive me and – restore me – and all my children
To the Paradise I left"

On the Theotokos

The *Spirit of* fire rent the flames
Amid the wheels of the chariot
When he came to Nazareth
And said, "Peace to you, Mary
Our Lord is with you, virgin"
Mary, the fruit – of your womb – shall bring to an end
The great shame of Adam's house

By the pray'r and petition
Of the holy virgin Mary
  Keep from us, O Son of God
  The scourge and the rod of wrath
  Grant us, O Lord, months of joy
Give us years of – abundance – and may our service
Be to your satisfaction

On the Saints

Come, let us all take refuge
In the apostles of our Lord
  Who by their suff'ring and pain
  Were pleasing to Christ, their Lord
  And they received His Spirit
And the keys of – the kingdom. - Throughout creation,
Their mem'ries are magnified

The martyrs hold in their hands
Sacred blood, which flowed from their necks
  They offer their blood and say,
  "See our blood, Lord, which was shed
  For we did not deny You,
As we suffered – for Your sake – do not turn away
from sinners who call on You

On One Saint

Bless'd is He who perfected
your martyrdom and wove your crown
  O most holy St. (Stephen)
  Behold, O noble athlete
  All the heights and all the depths
Rejoice in your – bless'd mem'ry – and offer praise to
the most Holy Trinity

On Repentance

"Open Your door of mercy"
The prodigal son cried aloud
  I have sinned against heaven
  and in Your sight, my Father,
  Accept me as Your poor slave
I am not e-ven worthy to be called Your son
God of mercy, forgive me!

Our times are much like ourselves
Our gen`e`ration is like us
The rich love this world's pleasures
And the poor lie in the dust
And men are like the serpents
Who dev`ou`er – each other – For they do not keep
God's judgment before their eyes

On the Departed

Bless'd is He who has confirmed
our hope in the Res`u`rrection
Paul witnesses to doubters
"O Foolish men, if the seed
Does not die it cannot live;
Thus He showed them – that the race – of Adam shall rise
from the dead in great glory

Remember the departed
who took Your Body and Blood, Lord
And received pardon through it
In the Zi`on in heaven.
And when You sit on Your throne,
To divide good – from evil – may they stand at Your
Right hand with faces unveiled

PETHGOMO

(Tone 8 – Chaarthum neethi…)

Your priests shall be clothed in righteousness / and Your saints in glory.

Halleluiah w'halleluiah.

For Your servant, David's sake, / turn not away the face of Your – anointed

The Lord swore to David,/ "In truth I will not turn away from you.

Halleluiah w'halleluiah

Of the fruit of your body/ I will set up-on your throne"…*Barekmor*

+ Glory be to the Father, Son and Holy Spirit

Unto the ages of ages and forevermore.

EQBO

(Shuchiyodu shudya beskudisha)

May the feet which stood in the
Holy place in purity
Tread the gates of Paradise
And abide with the angels...*Stoumen Kalos, Kurieleison*

QOLO

(Than kaipaniyaamaadhathe...)

God created Adam and
Sat down,- contemplating him
He saw how fair and like was
The Crea-ture to Creator
    The earthly one came and went
    Through the trees of Paradise
The angels marveled
At how- he was exalted...*Barekmor*

+ Glory be to the Father, Son and Holy Spirit

When Adam left Paradise
Weeping – and with his head bowed
The heavenly ones wept and
The trees – bowed their heads while the
    Seraphim shook their wings and
    Said, "How the exalted falls
Because he transgressed
The com-mandment of his Lord

Unto the ages of ages and forevermore.

Our Lord called out to Adam"
"Why do – you sleep in She`ol?"
The Son told Adam to rise
Adam – began to say thus:
    "How sweet and fair is this voice
    And how pleasant is its sound
This voice is like that
Which called – me among the trees"

Lord have mercy upon us and help us!

BO'UTHO of MOR JACOB

Son of – God, give – rest to Your priests among the just
In that – kingdom, - which has no end among the saints

The earth, - which was – their mother, was a bed for them
Their bo-dies were – clothed in the color of mourning
They did – not cease –to praise You by night and by day
O Lord, - grant them –to stand in joy at Your right hand

Because they were – strangers, may they be refreshed in
The marriage cham-ber of light, which is full of joy
They despised and – put away the fair crown of youth
They set their souls– against pleasures and loved Your name

Lord, let us not – hear that voice which cuts off all hope
We confess You – Acknowledge us and have mercy

*Turn to **Concluding Prayer of Matins (p. 23)***

THIRD HOUR of DAY SEVEN [Saturday]

Qaumo (p. 5)... Introductory Prayer (p. 24)

QOLO

(Lok Moriyo Qorenan/ Mochanamaacharyarkekuka Haleluiah)

O Lord, absolve Your clergy – Halleluiah.
The priests and deacons who served in their lifetime,
At Your altar in mon`a`steries – and churches,
They carried in their hands Your Body and Blood
For the pardon of their offences, O Lord God,
Forgive them – by Your true Body;
Absolve them – by Your holy Blood;
May they cry at Your right hand "Glory – to You Lord!"...*Barekmor*

+ Glory be to the Father, Son and Holy Spirit
Unto the ages of ages and forevermore.

How sweet is the word of our Lord which He spoke
To Simon, chief apostle, about the priesthood:
"I appoint you as the master of the house;
I have given you the keys of the heights and depths;
If you bind – I will also bind;
If you loose – I will also loose;
If you pray for sinners, then your pray'r – shall be heard."

Lord have mercy upon us and help us!

BO'UTHO of MOR JACOB

Son of God, give rest to Your priests among the just
In that kingdom which has no end among the saints

May the priests who have departed rejoice with You,
And be gladdened when You, O Christ, come in glory;
May our brothers and our teachers who passed from us
Be seated in Your Kingdom with all of Your saints.

The companies of priests on earth, O Lord Jesus,
Shall offer praises to You with halleluiahs,
Those whom You have taken from the Church upon earth;
Place them in the Church of the first-born in heaven.

Christ, who is the Lord of priests and the great High-Priest
Pardon, O Lord, Your priests, who served Your myst`eries.

Qaumo (p.5)

SIXTH HOUR of DAY SEVEN [Saturday]

Qaumo (p. 5)…Introductory Prayer (p. 25)

QOLO

(Phtah Li Tar`o Dahnonokh/ Kanyaka mariyaminekandu)

A new – heaven has appeared
On earth, the Virgin Mary;
See! The – Sun of righteousness,
Whose name is before the worlds,
  Shone forth from her on the world;
  Drove out the darkness of sin;
Bless`ed – is He who came forth
From her and magnified her…*Barekmor*

+ Glory be to the Father, Son and Holy Spirit

Peace be –unto the Prophets,
The Architects of the Faith;
Peace un-to the Apostles,
Builders of the Holy Church;
  Peace be unto the Martyrs
  Those who loved the Lord of peace;
Peace be – with the Holy Church,
Which honors their mem`o`ry.

Unto the ages of ages and forevermore.

Lord, mag-nify the mem'ry
Of Mary, Your Bless'd Mother
And the – Prophets, Apostles
Martyrs, the Just and Righteous
  Grant a place among them to
  The departed who consumed
Your Ho-ly Body and Blood
And have rested in Your hope
Lord have mercy upon us and help us!

Turn to ***Bo'utho of Mor Balai (p. 25)***

NINTH HOUR of DAY SEVEN [Saturday]

Qaumo (p. 5)... Introductory Prayer (p. 27)

QOLO

(Enono Nuhro Shareero/ Mekhathin gambheeradhwanipol)

The sound - of the last trumpet
Will be mighty like thunder
It will - not leave in She`ol
The odor of Adam's clay;
With one sound, it will raise up
The *entire* race of Adam,
Who shall be clothed in garments,
Which shall - never grow corrupt
In the new life forever...*Barekmor*

+ *Glory be to the Father, Son and Holy Spirit*
Unto the ages of ages and forevermore.

Do not - place me, my brothers
in a dec`o`rated grave
For I - am a grave, which is
Full of sins and offenses
Bury me among strangers
Where the poor are laid to rest
That when the Son of God comes
He may- call and raise me up
And have mercy upon me

Lord have mercy upon us and help us

BO'UTHO of MOR BALAI

Renew Your creatures by the res'rrection,
Your worshippers who have slept in Your hope.

Give rest and pardon to the dead, O Lord,
Who sleep in hope and await Your coming.

Lord, with Abraham, Isaac and Jacob,
Make Your servants rest, those who sleep in hope.

Their bodies and souls shall cry together:
"Bless'd is He who will come and raise the dead."

Qaumo (p. 5)

MAWRBE of NIGHT VIGIL

I

(1.2 – Lekh dithaikh, Deivathin maathave bhoolokathin)

You are the pride of the whole creation
O Theo-tokos
Because from you God the Word
Was pleased to take flesh
O virgin pure and holy,
We exalt you with praise

You are the closed door, which Ezek'el saw,
O Mother of God,
By which no man has entered
Except God the Word
O virgin pure and holy,
We exalt you with praise

You, who promised and said that where you are,
Your servants shall be
And all the martyrs heard You
And followed You, Lord
And shunned this temp`o`ral life
We exalt you with praise

O Lord, in your mercy give a good hope
To the de-parted
Who ate Your holy body
And absol – ving blood
Let them stand at Your right hand
When your majesty appears…*Barekmor*

+ Glory be to the Father, Son and the Holy Spirit
Unto the ages of ages and forevermore

Let us all offer praise to the Father
And worship the Son
And give thanks to the Spirit;
Three Holy Persons
Praise be to the One True God
And mercy be to us

II

(2.2 – Hoy d'Men Shmayone, Vaanavar doothar maanikunnole)

O you who are – extolled with wonder
By those above – and by those below
Peace to – you, Mother of God

You who gave birth – in virginity
And not by seed – but by the Spirit
Peace to – you, mother unwed

Peace be with you – O, you, Holy Saints
You friends of Christ – who trampled all pain
May your – pray'rs be our stronghold…*Barekmor*

+ Glory be to the Father, Son and the Holy Spirit
Unto the ages of ages and forevermore

When the watchers – exalt You with praise
As you descend – to bring the resurrection,
Lord, raise up the dead

III

(3.1 – Lekh d'kitho, Alavatonam deivathe)

O virgin, the God-bearer
Your body was glorified
For you were the treasure house.
By wonder, your womb carried
God Who is the infinite!
We all honor you!

The prophets foretold of you
By their myst'ries of wonder –
In the burning bush, the fleece,
The Ark of the Covenant,
The cloud, the lamp stand and the
Tablets of the law

We call on you, St. (Titus)
For we all are afflicted
Answer us, O holy one,
And respond to our requests
For your Lord loves you greatly
May your pray'r help us

Our Lord has given the pledge
Of life to the believers
That they pass from death to life
Bless`ed are the departed
Who ate His Body and Blood
For He will raise them…*Barekmor*

+Glory be to the Father, Son and the Holy Spirit
Unto the ages of ages and forevermore

The Church with all her children
Offers pure and pleasant praise
With sweet, melodi'ous voices
To the Father, and the Son,
And to the Holy Spirit;
We glorify Him!

IV

(4.3 – Lekh Fayo, Deivathin maathave)

O Virgin, God-bearer,
It is fitting to praise you
For it was through you God the Father reconciled
With our human race

Bless`ed are – You, O Lord
Who, in mercy, came to us
And who brought salvation and redemption for those
Who believed in You

The saints did – suffer pain
And all kinds of afflictions
O Lord of all, by your love may they intercede
For us all, sinners

The faithful – departed
Look for your second coming
That you might console them in the resurrection
And give thanks to You…*Barekmor*

+Glory be to the Father, Son and the Holy Spirit
Unto the ages of ages and forevermore

Holy are – You, O God,
Exalted forevermore;
Who placed the absolving altar by Your_ grace
In the Holy Church

V

(5.1 – Eshayo Duz kad hodeth, Kanyakagarbiniyayi athinal)

Exalt, Isaiah! Rejoice,
For the virgin has conceived
Behold, she has given birth – to the First – Born Son
He is truly God from God
We glorify and praise Him
He is the rad`i`ance and – the brightness
As the prophet spoke

Peace be unto you, Mary
The one who is full of grace
The prophets of the Spirit – were amazed – at you
Peace be unto you, O cloud
Which Isaiah prophesied
Peace be unto you, the staff – of Aaron –
Which brought forth new leaves

Exult, Fathers and teachers
And rejoice exceedingly
For the seed of your teaching – has sprouted – and grown
It has given fruits of faith
Thirty, sixty, *and* hundred fold,
According to the true Word – which was heard
In our Lord's Gospel

Grant rest and gladness to Your
Faithful servants, O Lord God
Console them as you promised – in resurrection
You, who were among the dead
And preached to them the Good News,
Raise the righteous ones who sleep – in Sheol –
From the destruction…*Barekmor*

+ Glory be to the Father, Son and the Holy Spirit

Unto the ages of ages and forevermore

The Church and all her children
Praise, adore, and glorify
The myst'ry, the Father, Son, - and Holy – Spirit:
The Father, True Light; the Son
The brilliance of His essence;
And the Comforter Spirit – One True God
We glorify Him

VI

(6.3 – Kad Mkad Menan, Deivathin maathave kanye vazthunnu)

When we draw near – to – you, Mary
To exult you, O Virgin
We glorify and praise Him
Who was born in flesh from you

We draw near to – You – Christ our God
To worship Your majesty
For by Your incarnation
You have enlightened the world

When we draw near – to – exult you
Prophets, apostles, *and* Martyrs,
We glorify and praise Him
For whom you endured suff'ring

We draw near to – you – departed
To pray and beseech the Lord
That our God may absolve you,
For you have slept in His hope…*Barekmor*

+ Glory be to the Father, Son and the Holy Spirit
Unto the ages of ages and forevermore

When we draw near – to – you, O Christ
We glorify and praise You,
And your heavenly Father,
And your all Holy Spirit

VII

(7.1 – Lhaw d'ethiled, Priyanam lazarinekabareen…)

Come, let us glorify Him who truly was born of the holy virgin
The Sun of Justice was manifested from the womb of Mary
Let us all – worship and – praise Him forever

Come, let us glorify Him who was born in the manger in Bethlehem
The One Who nourished thousands in the desert drank His mother's milk
Let us all – worship and – praise Him forever

Come, let us glorify Him who gave strength to the athletes in their battle
They fought against the evil one and they emerged in vict`o`ry
Let us all – worship and – praise Him forever

Come let us glorify Him who called Lazarus from the tomb and raised him,
And who saved the young man, son of the widow from the bonds of death
Let us all – worship and – praise Christ forever…*Barekmor*

+ Glory be to the Father, Son and the Holy Spirit
Unto the ages of ages and forevermore

Come let us glorify, worship, and offer praise to the Holy Father
Thanksgiving to His own Son and honor to the Holy Spirit
Let us all – worship and – praise Him forever

VIII

(8.1 – Yeldo Gnizo, Vishwasikal namme rakshipaan)

That invisible infant
Who appeared on Mount Horeb
Was seen in the burning bush
And came forth from the virgin – wondrously
To save and redeem us all
There-fore, we magnify her unceasingly

The bush beheld by Moses
Which the *fire* did not consume
Represented the Virgin
Who, without seed, gave birth to – God the Word
The creator of the world
There-fore, we magnify her unceasingly

The chosen twelve Apostles
Renounced the world and its snares
They despised earthly pleasures
And they put on Christ their God – their weapon
They have become our stronghold
There-fore, we magnify her unceasingly

In the dwellings of the saints
Who rejoice without ceasing;
In the tents of light, O Lord;
In the place of all Your saints – Christ our God,
Grant rest to all Your servants
Who have fallen asleep trusting in Your hope…*Barekmor*

+ Glory be to the Father, Son and the Holy Spirit
Unto the ages of ages and forevermore

Praise to the Holy Father
Who sent forth His Holy Son
Who dwelt in all holiness
In the pure and holy womb – of Mary
To save and redeem us all
There-fore, we magnify her unceasingly

PRAYER BEFORE SLEEP

Qaumo (p.5)
Introductory Prayer

O Merciful God, the voice of our prayer knocks at Your door. / Prevent not from Your worshippers the petitions of their needs. / We call upon You, O God, to assist us in our infirmities. / O Good One, hear the voice of our supplication and grant our petitions in Your mercy. Amin.

BO'UTHO of MOR EPHREM

Lord, have mercy upon us
O Lord receive our service
Send us from Your treasure-house
Mercy, grace, and forgiveness

Help me to keep vigil and
Stand watchfully before You
But if I were to slumber
May my sleep be without sin

If I sin while keeping watch
Lord, forgive me by Your grace
And if I sin in my sleep,
Absolve me by Your mercy!

O Lord, grant me peaceful sleep
By the Cross of Your meekness
Save me from all evil dreams
And from obscene images

While I sleep throughout this night
Lord, protect me and prevent
Evil men and sinful thoughts
From taking control of me

Send me an angel of light
To protect my whole body
By Your flesh which I've consumed
Save me from hateful passions

Lord, when I lie down to sleep
May Your blood be my guardian
Granting freedom to my soul
Which is formed in Your image

Overshadow my body
With Your right hand, which formed it
May Your fortress of mercy
Be a shield surrounding me

May Your strength be my guardian
As my body sleeps in peace
May that sleep be like incense
Before Your great majesty

By the pray'rs of Your Mother
Let not Satan near my bed
By Your sacrifice for me
Forbid him from harming me

Lord, fulfill what You promised
Guard my life by Your Cross that
I may praise You when I wake
For you loved my feebleness

Grant, by Your compassion, Lord
That I may obey Your will
Grant us an evening of peace
And a night of righteousness

Christ our Savior, O True Light
Whose honor dwells in the light
You are indeed the True Light
Whom the sons of light worship

Jesus, Savior of the world
Who dwells truly in the light
Have mercy upon us in
This world and the world to come

Glory to You! Praise to You!
Thousands of praises to You
Glory Lord! Glory to You,
Lord, have mercy on us all

Praise the One Watchers worship
Praise the One the angels serve
Lord of Watchers and angels
Hear the pleas of Your faithful

Praise Him Who is one essence
Praise Him Who is three persons
Father, Son, Holy Spirit
Who is the One and True God

Glory to Him who accepts
Like first-fruits and off`e`rings
The tears of the penitent
And the pray'rs of the feeble

Countless as the leaves of trees
Are those on earth who praise You
Whom Watchers in Heaven serve
And whom angels glorify

With wisdom and purity
Let us glorify our God
Father, Son, Holy Spirit
Who is the one and true God

* *These verses are used during the Fast of Nineveh and of the Great Fast*

Do not keep gold and silver
Which contain deadly poison
Rather, obtain sound doctrine
That you are loved by the Lord

Observe the forty-days' fast
And give bread to the hungry
And as you learned from David
Pray seven times every day (Ps 119:164)

Both Moses and Elijah
Fasted forty days and nights
As our Lord also fasted
And conquered the evil one

May the pray'r which ascended
From the furnace, sea and pit
Open the door of mercy
For our pray'r and petition

Lord, who hears our petitions
Answer us in Your mercy
Lord, be reconciled with us
Have compassion upon us

***[Psalm 4]* O God, the salvation of my righteousness, You have answered me when I called/ You have comforted me in my affliction. / Have mercy upon me and hear my prayer.**

O sons of men, how long will you hide my honour? /How long will you love vanity and seek after lies? / Know that the Lord has wondrously set apart the chosen one. / The Lord will hear when I call to Him.

Be angry, but do not sin. / Meditate within your hearts and upon your beds / Offer sacrifices of righteousness and put your trust in the Lord.

There are many who say: / "Who will show us any good and shed the light of His face upon us?"
O Lord, You have placed Your joy in my heart, / more than the time when their grain, wine, and oil abounded.

In peace I will lie down and sleep. / For You alone, O Lord, make me dwell in tranquility./ And to You belongs the praise, O God. / Barekmor.

O Holy Father, guard us by Your sacred name.

O Son of God, our Savior, protect us with Your victorious Cross.
O Holy Spirit, make us worthy temples of Your holy habitation.
O Lord our God, forever shelter us under Your divine wings at all times forever, Amin.

INTERCESSORY PRAYERS - QUQLION

COMMEMORATION of the MOTHER of GOD - QUQLION

Pethgomo

(Ninnal stuthiyodu rajamakal...)

The King's daughter stands in glory - Halleluiah
And the Queen at - Your right hand.

Leave your people and your father's house - Halleluiah
For the King will desire - your beauty...*Barekmor*

+ Glory be to the Father, Son and Holy Spirit
Unto the ages of ages and forevermore.

Eqbo

(Bhakthar pukazhcha...)

O Pride of the faithful ones
Offer pray'rs on our behalf
To the Only Begotten
That he have mercy on us - *Stoumen kalos, Kurielaison*

Qolo - Option 1

(Mannamakalkayi..)

Gabriel brought Peace to the
Daughter of David
And said, "The Lord is with you,
And shall come forth from you. *Barekmor.*

+ Glory be to the Father, Son and the Holy Spirit
Unto the ages of ages and forevermore.

Like a ship, Mary carried,
Adored, and honored
The Captain Who is the Lord
Of all creation
Lord have mercy upon us and help us

OR

Qolo - Option 2
(Mariamin smaranam)

May Mary's Mem'ry
Be for our blessing
May her pray'r be a
Fortress for our souls. *Barekmor.*

+ Glory be to the Father, Son and the Holy Spirit
Unto the ages of ages and forevermore.

Behold, sweet fragrance
Rises in the air
For Virgin Mary
The Theotokos
Lord have mercy upon us and help us

OR

Qolo - Option 3
(Sweekaranam nedi...)

Virgin, chosen to
Be the Mother of God
Through whom the curse was
Uprooted – from Earth
Pray to your Son that
Peace and concord may be
Poured upon His Church
Throughout all the world. Barekmor.

+ Glory be to the Father, Son and Holy Spirit
Unto the ages of ages and forevermore.

Glory to the Pow'r
Who left the Cherubim
And the Seraphim,
Descending to dwell
In the Virgin's womb;
And He took flesh from her
To save Adam's sons
From Death and Satan
Lord have mercy upon us and help us

OR

Qolo - Option 4

(Deivathin maatha...)

May mem'ry be made of the Mother of God
With the Prophets, Apostles, and the Martyrs
And the Children of the Church upon the earth
May Good mem'ry be made now and forever. Barekmor.

+ *Glory be to the Father, Son and Holy Spirit*
Unto the ages of ages and forevermore.

Glory to the Son of God Who willed to come
From the womb of the Blessed Virgin Mary
And saved the people from error, by His Birth
Exalting her mem'ry; may her pray'rs help us.
Lord have mercy upon us and help us.

Bo'utho – Option 1

(Moraneeshu kurishum nee...)

By Your Cross, our Lord Jesus
And the pray'r of Your Mother
Keep from us all afflictions,
Punishments, and rods of wrath

OR

Bo'utho - Option 2

(Nirtheedaruthe parishudhe...)

O Holy One, do not cease
Your intercession for us
To your only Begotten
That He have mercy on us

COMMEMORATION OF THE SAINTS – QUQLION

Pethgomo
(Nayavan panapole...)

The righteous shall flourish like a palm tree - Halleluiah
Like cedars of Lebanon – they shall grow.

They shall flourish and be great in old age - Halleluiah
They shall be fruitful – and fragrant…*Barekmor.*

+ Glory be to the Father, Son and Holy Spirit
Unto the ages of ages and forevermore.

Eqbo
(Orupolingum...)

Your mem'ry O St. (Thomas)
Be kept here and in Heaven
May your pray'r be a help to
Those who honor your mem'ry. *Stoumen kalos, Kurielaison*

Qolo - Option 1
(Prarthanayin samayamithallo...)

Behold, the time of prayer, (O St. Thomas)
Stand and intercede at the head of your flock
Stretch forth your hand like Moses and bless all those
Who hasten to the sound of your gentle voice…*Barekmor*

+ Glory be to the Father, Son and the Holy Spirit
Unto the ages of ages and forevermore.

Praise to the Father Who chose you, St. (Thomas)
And to the Son Who honors your memory
Worshipped is the Holy Spirit Who crowns you
By your pray'rs, may mercy be on us always
Lord have mercy upon us and help us

OR

Qolo - Option 2
(Bhagyam nibiyarkum...)

Bless'd are the Prophets,
And the Apostles
Bless'd are the Martyrs
At Resurrection. *Barekmor*

+ Glory be to the Father, Son and the Holy Spirit
Unto the ages of ages and forevermore.

Martyrs who desired
To behold the Christ
By the sword, gained wings,
And flew to the heights
Lord have mercy upon us and help us

OR

Qolo - Option 3
(Lokarkupakaram...)

Peace, O chosen one!
Merchant of the universe;
Great treasury – who gives help to all
Heal those who are sick
Cleanse those with evil spirits
By your pray'rs may – we receive mercy. Barekmor

+ Glory be to the Father, Son and Holy Spirit
Unto the ages of ages and forevermore.

Glory be to Christ
At the Feast of St. (Thomas)
Who worked for truth – and fulfilled justice;
Who endured torments
And kept vigil, fast, and pray'r
For the hope of – everlasting life
Lord have mercy upon us and help us

OR

Qolo - Option 4
(N'beeye qadeeshe)

O Holy Prophets,
Apostles, the Kingdom's sons
Pray that we not drown
In the raging sea of sin. Barekmor

+ Glory be to the Father, Son and Holy Spirit
Unto the ages of ages and forevermore.

O Holy Martyrs
The servants of God Most High
May your prayers for us
Be a fortress and refuge
Lord have mercy upon us and help us

Bo'utho – Option 1
(Parishudhanmare ningal...)

Pray for us, O Holy Saints
To Him Whose will you fulfilled,
Keep from us all afflictions,
Punishments, and rods of wrath.

OR

Bo'utho - Option 2
(Mar Thoma salguna nidhiye...)

O Resplendent St. (Thomas)
May the concord of your Lord
And His peace flow in the Church
Which forever honors you

COMMEMORATION of the DEPARTED CLERGY - QUQLION

Pethgomo
(Charthum neethi...)

Your priests shall be clothed in righteousness/ and Your saints in glory.
Halleluiah vu halleluiah
For Your servant, David's sake, /turn not away the face of Your – anointed

The Lord swore to David,/ "in truth I will not turn away from you.
Halleluiah vu halleluiah
Of the fruit of your body/ I will set upon your throne". *Barekmor*

+ Glory be to the Father, Son and Holy Spirit
Unto the ages of ages and forevermore.

Eqbo

(Suchiyodu shudhya)

May the feet which stood in the
Holy place in purity
Tread the gates of Paradise
And abide with the angels. *Stoumen Kalos, Kurieleison*

Qolo – Option 1

(Nirmala madhbahayil...)

O Lord, lead to Your Kingdom
With the angels of heaven,
Those priests who have ministered
Your mystr'ies at the altar. *Barekmor.*

+ Glory be to the Father, Son and the Holy Spirit
Unto the ages of ages and forevermore.

Son of God, forget them not,
Those priests who have served You well
Lord, grant them unveiled faces
On the day of Your coming.
Lord have mercy upon us and help us

OR

Qolo - Option 2

(Deivom strishtichaadathe...)

God created Adam and
Sat down, contemplating him
He saw how fair and like the
Creature was to Creator
The earthly one came and went
Through the trees of Paradise
The angels marveled
At how he was exalted. *Barekmor.*

+ Glory be to the Father, Son and Holy Spirit
Unto the ages of ages and forevermore.

Moses and Aaron received
The priesthood which was passed down
It went to Zachariah
Then it was given to John
John then gave it to our Lord
Who ordained the apostles
And the apostles
Spread it throughout creation.
Lord have mercy upon us and help us

OR

Qolo Option 3

(Mochanam acharyarkekuka...)

O Lord, absolve Your clergy, Halleluiah
The priests and deacons who served in their lifetime
At Your altar in monasteries – and churches
They carried in their hands Your body and blood
For the pardon of their offenses – O Lord, by
Your body – absolve their debts and
By Your blood – forgive all their sins
May they cry at Your right hand, "Glory – to You Lord!" *Barekmor.*

+ Glory be to the Father, Son and Holy Spirit
Unto the ages of ages and forevermore.

How sweet is the word of our - Lord which He spoke
To Simon, chief Apostle, about – the priesthood:
"I have made you the master - of the house and
Given to your hands the keys of the – heights and depths
If you bind - that I will bind and
If you loose – that I will loose and
If you pray for sinners your pray-er – shall be heard."
Lord have mercy upon us and help us

Bo'utho – Option 1

(Achyaresha…)

Christ Who is the Lord of priests and the great High Priest
Pardon, O Lord, Your priests who served Your myst`eries

OR

Bo'utho - Option 2
(Mudikal madanjotti thakidum…)

Crowns are plaited and arranged
Upon the holy altar
To be placed on every priest
Who has served in purity

COMMEMORATION of the FAITHFUL DEPARTED - QUQLION

Pethgomo
(Makalilappan...)

As a father shows mercy to his children - Halleluiah
So the Lord shows mercy to those – who fear him

As for man, his days are like grass, - Halleluiah
Like the flow`er of the field – so he blooms…*Barekmor*

+ Glory be to the Father, Son and Holy Spirit
Unto the ages of ages and forevermore.

Eqbo
(Sharanathale...)

May Your Living voice awake
From the graves to Paradise
Your servants who slept in hope
And trusted in Your mercy. *Stoumen kalos, Kurielaison.*

Qolo - Option 1
(Rakshakane nin gathrathe...)

O Savior, raise up the dead who ate Your Flesh
And drank Your Blood, the Chalice of Salvation
Raise them up from the grave without corruption
And clothe them in glory, those who wait – for You. *Barekmor.*

+ Glory be to the Father, Son and the Holy Spirit
Unto the ages of ages and forevermore.

The Son of the King who gives life to the dead
Will be carried above the clouds of beauty
The righteous who hear the trumpet before him
Will be clothed in glorious garments and meet him
Lord have mercy upon us and help us

OR

Qolo - Option 2
(Uyierekunon raja...)

The Life-Giving King
Shall appear in His glory
To restore life - to the departed
From graves they will rise
To offer praise together
To the One Who - gives life to the dead. *Barekmor.*

+ Glory be to the Father, Son and the Holy Spirit
Unto the ages of ages and forevermore.

How sweet are the words
Our Lord spoke in His Gospel:
"He who receives – My Body and Blood
Shall not be left in
She`ol for I tasted death
That he may have- everlasting life"
Lord have mercy upon us and help us

OR

Qolo - Option 3
(Nadha thavakairulokam...)

Your authority, O Lord
Is present in both the worlds
Keep the living by Your Cross
And absolve the faithful dead. *Barekmor.*

+ Glory be to the Father, Son and Holy Spirit
Unto the ages of ages and forevermore.

Glory to You Who gives life
To those who lie in the tombs
Glory be to Your Father
And to the Holy Spirit.
Lord have mercy upon us and help us

Bo'utho – Option 1
(Maramathinuyare...)

O Lord, may the departed
Who confessed the Trinity
Be received in Your kingdom
As was promised to the thief

OR

Bo'uto Option 2
(Than maranathal...)

Son of God, who by Your death
Quickened our mortality
Give us life from the dust that
We may cry: "Glory to You!"

COMMEMORATION of the HOLY CROSS - QUQLION

Pethgomo
(Vellum shathrukale…)

Through You we shall strike down our enemies – Halleluiah
In Your name we shall trample - on our foes

You have saved us from our foes – Halleluiah
And have put to shame all our - enemies. *Barekmor*

+ Glory be to the Father, Son and Holy Spirit
Unto the ages of ages and forevermore.

Eqbo
(Sleeba Vennu Vellunu)

The Cross conquered and conquers
The Cross has conquered Satan
May the Cross be a stronghold
To all who confess the Cross…*Stoumen Kalos, Kurieleison*

Qolo – Option 1

(Nathan kootayul athinaal)

We fear not the evil one
Because the Lord is with us
We are clothed in His armor
And in it we all glory…*Barekmor*

+ Glory be to the Father, Son and the Holy Spirit
Unto the ages of ages and forevermore.

May He, who carried the Cross
On his shoulder from Zion,
Sprinkle His dew of mercy
Upon the bones of the dead.
Lord have mercy upon us and help us.

OR

Qolo – Option 2

(Sleebaye vandipathinal…)

From Rome, the city of kings, to Je-rusalem
Helena the Queen arrived – to adore the Cross
She asked the Jews - to lead her to it
They answered her - "Go seek the rabbi."
If you take hold of him he will show you the place
Where the Cross, which you have been seeking is buried.
Halleluiah – the Cross of our Lord. *Barekmor*

+ Glory be to the Father, Son and the Holy Spirit
Unto the ages of ages and forevermore.

Our God, Emmanuel, was - hung upon the wood
The Son of the Almighty - bowed His head and died
Upon the wood – his spirit left him
But his essence – left not his body
Our Lord left His earthly life – Not His *e-ternal one*
For having crucified Him – the Jews will repent
Halleluiah – O Lord have mercy!
Lord have mercy upon us and help us.

Qolo – Option 3

(Moonam maniyilumenerathum)

At the third hour and at all times we shall worship –
the life-giving Cross
And we sign ourselves with it for it is our hope –
and strong protection
By day and night - it delivers us from Satan
and his powers. *Barekmor*

+ *Glory be to the Father, Son and the Holy Spirit*
Unto the ages of ages and forevermore.

With his staff Moses divided the Red Sea and -
Isr'el passed over
By the Cross of light our Lord did open Sheol –
and raised up the dead
Blessed is Christ – who trod for us the way of *life from* –
the grave to Paradise
Lord have mercy upon us and help us

Bo'utho – Option 1

(Sleeba varuzhuka swargathil)

May the Cross which reigns in heav'n
The same cross which reigns on earth
Be a stronghold for all the
Churches and monasteries

OR

Bo'utho – Option 2

(Yerusalem Gogulthayil)

Glory to Jesus who was
Crucified on Golgotha
He cried out and rocks were split
The dead rose and sang praises